Leading With Values

As societies become more polarized, there is increasing pressure for business leaders to have a sense of purpose and to make moral decisions. Being a good leader requires both a keen understanding of the realities of human decision-making as well as an analysis of what is right and wrong. This book integrates lessons from three intellectual traditions – psychology, philosophy, and political economy – to guide readers on a journey to rigorously explore their values and decision-making. The authors begin by examining people's intuitions about right and wrong. Then they clarify principles that embody these intuitions and help readers engage with others whose intuitions or principles differ from their own. Ultimately, this book teaches readers how to be strategic as they lead with their values: as individuals, as designers of organizations, and as businesspeople interacting with societal institutions.

Neil Malhotra is the Edith M. Cornell Professor of Political Economy at Stanford Graduate School of Business.

Ken Shotts is the David S. and Ann M. Barlow Professor of Political Economy at Stanford Graduate School of Business.

Leading With Values

Strategies for Making Ethical Decisions in Business and Life

NEIL MALHOTRA

Stanford Graduate School of Business

KEN SHOTTS

Stanford Graduate School of Business

Shaftesbury Road, Cambridge CB2 8EA, United Kingdom

One Liberty Plaza, 20th Floor, New York, NY 10006, USA

477 Williamstown Road, Port Melbourne, VIC 3207, Australia

314–321, 3rd Floor, Plot 3, Splendor Forum, Jasola District Centre, New Delhi – 110025, India

103 Penang Road, #05–06/07, Visioncrest Commercial, Singapore 238467

Cambridge University Press is part of Cambridge University Press & Assessment, a department of the University of Cambridge.

We share the University's mission to contribute to society through the pursuit of education, learning and research at the highest international levels of excellence.

www.cambridge.org
Information on this title: www.cambridge.org/9781108841191
DOI: 10.1017/9781108893220

First published 2022 (version 3, March 2024)

Printed in Great Britain by CPI Group (UK) Ltd, Croydon CR0 4YY

A catalogue record for this publication is available from the British Library.

Library of Congress Cataloging-in-Publication Data
Names: Malhotra, Neil Ankur, author. | Shotts, Kenneth W., author.
TITLE: Leading with values : strategies for making ethical decisions in business and life / Neil Malhotra, Stanford Graduate School of Business, Ken Shotts, Stanford Graduate School of Business.
DESCRIPTION: New York : Cambridge University Press, 2022. | Includes bibliographical references and index.
IDENTIFIERS: LCCN 2021039461 (print) | LCCN 2021039462 (ebook) | ISBN 9781108841191 (hardback) | ISBN 9781108789752 (paperback) | ISBN 9781108893220 (epub)
SUBJECTS: LCSH: Business ethics. | Leadership–Moral and ethical aspects. | Values. | BISAC: BUSINESS & ECONOMICS / Business Ethics
CLASSIFICATION: LCC HF5387 .M3338 2022 (print) | LCC HF5387 (ebook) | DDC 174/.4–dc23
LC record available at https://lccn.loc.gov/2021039461
LC ebook record available at https://lccn.loc.gov/2021039462

ISBN 978-1-108-84119-1 Hardback

For Jane and Sylvie – Neil Malhotra
For Rachel and Maureen – Ken Shotts

Contents

Figures and Tables

Figures

Tables

Acknowledgments

This book builds on decades of accumulated institutional knowledge at the Stanford Graduate School of Business (GSB), and we owe a deep debt of gratitude to our colleagues and students.

Over the years, we have taught versions of the GSB's core ethics class with many colleagues: Jon Bendor, Dave Brady, Ernesto Dal Bo, Saumitra Jha, Scotty McLennan, Romain Wacziarg, and Justin Wolfers. From them we have learned a tremendous amount about cases, theories, and pedagogy. Among our colleagues, four deserve particular mention: Dave Baron, who laid a foundation for teaching normative ethics and business–society relations in his classic textbook *Business and Its Environment*; Keith Krehbiel, who spearheaded the effort to bring descriptive ethics and psychology into the ethics curriculum; Benoît Monin, who worked closely with us for much of the past decade as we taught and refined the material; and Sheila Melvin, who worked with us to develop several cases that we draw on in the book. Our class is what it is, and this book is what it is, in large part due to what we have learned from them.

We also have learned from our students. Our PhD course assistants and graders have helped us be more precise about the material and how it applies to concrete situations. Our MBA, MSx, and executive students have given us an enormous amount of feedback about how to make ethics more engaging and impactful. Even when that feedback was blunt and critical it was ultimately incredibly useful, and many of our teaching techniques and applications were inspired by their suggestions. Over the years, their increasing engagement and enthusiasm for the class have inspired us to continually work to make it better. We are especially grateful to the following group of MBA1s who, in the midst of the COVID-19 pandemic, took the time to participate in a focus group and give us feedback on the completed manuscript: Alex Bennett, Cara Eckholm, Adam Keppler, Eliza LaJoie, Evan Mendez, Sam Pressler, Joan Thompson, and Melissa Zhang.

We also received helpful comments from Mykel Kochenderfer and Jeff Berner on aerospace engineering and from Jon Levin and Paul Oyer on the role of business in society. Several of our colleagues (Anat Admati, Dave Baron, Jon Bendor, Keith Krehbiel, Scotty McLennan, Cristian Mendoza Ovando, Benoît Monin, and Paul Pfleiderer) generously provided detailed and thoughtful comments on the entire manuscript. Their generosity with their time, and their willingness to engage with us, even on points of disagreement, has helped us sharpen our thinking and writing. Of course, any mistakes that remain are solely our own responsibility.

We are immensely grateful to Robert Dreesen, who provided tremendous insights, encouragement, and support throughout the writing process. We are also thankful for terrible Chicago rush-hour traffic. Neil and Robert initially discussed the idea for this book while stuck in an Uber together on the way to O'Hare International Airport. Lastly, we greatly appreciate the helpful comments from anonymous reviewers as well the team at Cambridge University Press.

From Neil: I thank my parents for everything they have selflessly invested in me. Among my many friends, I want to highlight seven who comprise WhatsApp threads that resulted in much procrastination while writing this book: Alex Kuo and Luke Condra (the "Circus Circus" thread); Brad Simmons, Nick Simmons, and Tony Mataya (the "Hi." thread); Sujay Jaswa and Vipin Narang (the "Covid 2020" thread). During the period of isolation and social distancing during which this book was written, the humor, intellectual debate, and emotional support from those threads carried me through. Further, many of the topics, arguments, and turns of phrase in this book drew inspiration from those virtual discussions. I thank Jim Na and the rest of my poker buddies for providing much needed distraction and relaxation while putting aside the manuscript.

Finally, and most importantly, I want to thank Jane and Sylvie, who are my entire world. Thank you for your understanding while I spent time on this book that could have been spent with you. Thank you for embodying the values to which I aspire and from which I draw inspiration. And thank you for making me want to be a better man.

From Ken: I thank my parents, Wayne, Jacki, and Melinda, as well as Aunt Carolynn. Both as a child and as an adult I have always felt incredibly loved and have been inspired by your examples of living by your values. Throughout my education, I have been fortunate to learn from gifted teachers of descriptive, normative, and societal ethics, including Martha Edelman, Jack Schiemann, and Debra Satz. I also thank my brother and my friends from 553 for always being there and for their warm mockery of my academic writing (hopefully they never get their hands on this book).

While writing this book in the era of COVID-19, the only people I've been able to spend much time with are Rachel and Maureen. I wouldn't have it any other way. Even more than in normal times, I feel so fortunate to be with you, doing everyday things like baking, reading, hiking, and watching *The Office*. Rachel, one of the things that I admire most about you is your commitment to living by your values, even when it's difficult or inconvenient. Maureen, I'm proud to see you defining your own strong, independent values and pushing Rachel and me to reexamine our own. I look forward to continuing this journey together.

1

Core Values

Why We Lead, Why We Follow

In the summer of 1997, Apple Computer was struggling and on the verge of bankruptcy. The stock was trading at $3.56 per share. The company's last blockbuster product was the Macintosh personal computer in 1984, and since then the Microsoft operating system and IBM PC clones had established market dominance. In a desperate move, Apple decided to bring back cofounder Steve Jobs as CEO, twelve years after he was ousted from Apple in a power struggle with then-CEO John Sculley.

Dressed in cargo shorts, Birkenstock sandals, and his trademark black shirt, Jobs addressed his employees shortly before the launch of the iMac and the "Think Different" advertising campaign.[1] This was in the midst of the dot-com boom of the late 1990s, when Apple engineers could have deserted the company to join one of the many hot startups in Silicon Valley. Employees were likely excited by Jobs's return, but also uncertain.

Jobs's speech is now famous in Silicon Valley circles:

To me, marketing is about values ... Our customers want to know: Who is Apple and what is it that we stand for? Where do we fit in this world? And what we are about isn't making boxes for people to get their jobs done, although we do that well. We do that better than almost anybody in some cases. But Apple's about something more than that. Apple at the core – its core value is that we believe that people with passion can change the world for the better.

Jobs's point is that core values are central to why people buy a product. His articulation of Apple's central core value – captured in its famous "Think Different" campaign – is basically this: Albert Einstein, Martin Luther King Jr., Amelia Earhart, John Lennon, and Mahatma Gandhi would have used Apple products. Apple celebrates iconoclastic,

1

disruptive, rebellious thinkers and doers who change the world for the better. It's not a company for worker drones. And Apple customers and employees like to think of themselves this way as well. Without this set of core values, it is unlikely that people would be willing to pay large price premiums for Macs, iPhones, iPads, and Apple Watches.

Jobs said that marketing is about core values, but we will go further. The fundamental premise of this book is that *leadership is about core values*. To be an effective leader, you need to be someone others want to follow. People follow others for many reasons – because they are dynamic, competent, or charismatic. Yet, what makes a leader most compelling are their values. People are inspired by leaders whose decisions are based on a core set of values that resonate.

"Think Different" was a great advertising campaign, but Apple's customers weren't the most important audience for Jobs's speech. They weren't even in the room. The key audiences were investors, engineers, and managers, who cared deeply about the direction of the company. When Jobs returned as CEO, he articulated a vision for how he would lead, and what the company was all about. Under his leadership, Apple launched a string of revolutionary products, and by 2011 it was the most valuable publicly traded company in the world.

That same year, at the age of fifty-six, Steve Jobs died of pancreatic cancer. People spontaneously gathered in front of his house in Palo Alto and at Apple stores around the world to mourn and to place flowers, notes, candles, and, yes, apples.[2] That's not the normal reaction to the death of a business tycoon. In some ways it felt more like the death of a beloved pop star, princess, or prophet.

But not everyone was ready to nominate Jobs for sainthood. According to multiple books and articles drawing on firsthand accounts of his behavior, his managerial style left a lot to be desired.[3] Like many visionaries, he was a deeply flawed human being.

Apple's corporate conduct also came under intense scrutiny. The company's products were criticized for being environmentally destructive, addictive for users, and designed for premature obsolescence. The company's use of offshoring to dodge taxes was criticized as a selfish way of taking advantage of loopholes in the tax code. The company was caught colluding with Google and others in a "no poaching" agreement to hold down wages of engineers. Most serious, and most damaging, were criticisms of Apple's supply chain. Labor rights activists alleged that Foxconn and other key suppliers in China relied on child labor, coercion, punishingly long hours, low wages, and brutal working conditions. Multiple workers committed suicide by jumping off the top of company dormitories at the factories that manufactured Apple's stylish, elegantly designed iPhones.[4]

The criticisms of Apple have been hotly debated, and our goal in mentioning them is not to definitively assess the company's behavior. Rather, our point is to note that the criticisms were fundamentally driven by *values*. So values aren't just for personal leadership. They are also central for leadership of companies at a time when customers, employees, governments, and citizens increasingly care about how they affect society, not simply whether they make money for their shareholders. A company's standing and reputation depend crucially on its values. Like many great leaders, Jobs left behind a complex legacy that was quite messy because of conflicts over values.

At Apple, the criticisms did not go unnoticed. Tim Cook, who took over as CEO during the final stages of Jobs's battle with cancer, set a markedly different tone for the company's relationship with society. In part, he did this by publicly articulating the company's longstanding commitments to values such as LGBT rights and user privacy. The company also made substantial changes to its business practices. It ramped up its efforts to monitor and improve conditions in its suppliers' factories. And it made major strides in its environmental impacts, to the point that Greenpeace, which had previously been quite critical, rated it as the world's most environmentally friendly tech company.[5]

For Apple, which now ranks among the most admired companies in the world, values aren't just about the design or marketing of the company's products. They're also about how the company relates to society.

VALUES AND LEADERSHIP

What are values? They are beliefs and convictions about what is important in life and how to live and interact with others. They can help us decide right from wrong, guide the best way to live, and choose one action over another. At a deeper level, they determine our answers to big-picture questions about our lives and careers: What do you want to be known for? When you die, how do you want to be remembered? While you're alive, how do you want to relate to people around you? How do you want your company to treat its employees and customers? What sort of impact do you want to have in the world?

For many people, values are deeply personal. Your values may be based on strong religious convictions. They may be influenced by philosophy, stories, and literature. They probably stem from cultural traditions. They may reflect your family history and life experiences, especially those involving loss, struggle, or injustice. And they may build on what you've learned from your loved ones. Each person has their own story and path that leads to their personal values.

Because they come from so many different sources, values are inherently *subjective*: they are personally held and people do not all agree on one "correct" set of values. However, values are also, in the words of the historian Yuval Noah Harari, *inter-subjective*: Each person's values are commonly held by some others as well.[6] This is what gives values their power – they aren't just the quirky tastes of individuals, but rather are deeply meaningful to groups of people defined by cultures, religions, nations, and organizations. Of course, this also makes leading with values challenging, because groups of people can disagree about values. One group's values can be viewed as deeply problematic, and even abhorrent, from the perspective of others.

Fortunately, organizations don't require perfect alignment on values in order to succeed. Effective leaders are those who, in the absence of perfect alignment, are adept at identifying commonalities and building on them. Leaders are successful if they can understand and communicate their own core values, persuade their followers (while at the same time being open to persuasion), and manage value conflicts among people in their organizations. This book is about leading organizations with our values – that is, with principle and purpose. Doing so not only makes leaders more ethical, it also makes them more effective.

Although we will focus mainly on examples from the business world, this book is meant for anyone who leads other people. In addition to CEOs of large corporations, this includes military officers, teachers, high school basketball coaches, ministers, product managers, doctors, and many others. Understanding one's own values is crucial regardless of the scale of leadership. And the central lessons of this book apply within any sort of organizational structure, including governments and nonprofits.

OUR APPROACH

This book is the product of our experiences at the Stanford Graduate School of Business (GSB), where, for the past decade, we have developed and taught a required class on business ethics for MBAs and mid-career

Master's students, as well as sessions on values-based leadership for senior executives.

Business ethics isn't high on most people's list of classes they want to take. Indeed, the concept of business ethics might strike you as an oxymoron, a hopeless cause, a fig leaf for greedy capitalists, a boring academic version of compliance training, a vehicle for politically correct indoctrination, or an unrealistic fantasy of a world without tradeoffs. If you have any of these reactions, you're not alone. Coming into our class, many of our students have them too.

But over the years we've seen that, although our students are skeptical, and although they seek wealth, power, and success (after all, they're in business school!), the overwhelming majority of them have a strong desire to live and lead according to their values. They also want to understand each other's values, including those they disagree with. When they graduate, they want to join companies and take on roles that are consistent with their core values. And over the course of their careers they want to build and lead companies and organizations that embody their values and have positive impacts on society. To gain admission to the Stanford GSB, one must answer the following essay question: "What matters most to you, and why?" In many ways, this is the central question any leader – indeed, any human – must answer. People's answers to this question are constantly evolving, a journey rather than a fixed destination.

Our goal in this book, as in our class, is simple: to help you think about values and act and lead according to them. To do this, we will explore values at four levels.

- At a *personal* level, we will help you examine your own values and commitments, where they come from, and what they imply for your career and life decisions.
- At an *interpersonal* level, we will help you understand the values of others, as well as the emotional, rational, and cultural underpinnings of those values.
- At an *organizational* level, we will analyze how rules, incentives, and informal norms influence people's actions, and even their values.
- At a *societal* level, we will analyze how social institutions embody values, not just by setting limits on acceptable behavior, but also by structuring companies' incentives to respect or ignore the well-being of different stakeholders.

In addition to exploring values, this book is about how to act and lead with them. For this, good intentions aren't enough. It's also crucial to use effective strategies. There are many different ways to lead with your values, and the approach that works best for you will depend on your personality, your role, your culture, your organization, and the values themselves. That said, throughout this book, we will offer tips and pointers that our students have found useful and that we hope will also be useful for you. To be clear, these strategies are not cookie-cutter recipes, but rather guidelines to help you develop you own, personalized leadership and organizational plan.

At a personal level, we will consider strategies and habits for living your life and making decisions in accordance with your values. At an interpersonal level, we will discuss how to articulate your views to others while respecting their convictions. At an organizational level, we will discuss how to design institutions to encourage people to adhere to a company's values. And at a societal level, we will analyze strategies for interacting with stakeholders and governments in ways that are both effective and ethical.

When we say that leadership is about core values, we do not mean to suggest there aren't other important aspects of being an effective leader. Entire books have been written about power, empathy, creativity, delegation, negotiation, and resilience, among many other topics. The goal of this book is not to cover every aspect of leadership. Rather, we focus on core values because they have become an increasingly important aspect of leadership in society.

INTELLECTUAL FOUNDATIONS

In this book we will use two sets of tools to understand values-based leadership: *descriptive ethics* and *normative ethics*. Descriptive (or behavioral) ethics is the study of how people actually make ethical choices. The focus is not on whether a course of action is right or wrong, but rather on *why* people make the ethical choices they do in business settings. Descriptive ethics is rooted in moral and social psychology, but also touches on fields such as cultural anthropology, as it has been argued that humans' moral nature is rooted in both evolution and cultural transmission. Descriptive ethics can help you understand actions of key stakeholders whose motivations stem from moral concerns, predict how others may evaluate your actions, and increase your self-awareness of how you react in various situations. The psychological constraints of ethical decision-making help us understand why people sometimes make bad decisions that are inconsistent with their values.

We will also discuss normative ethics, which is the study of what makes an action (or a person) ethical or unethical. Normative ethics is the study of values, drawing from numerous traditions: art, literature, religion, and philosophy. Although we will not cover all possible values, we will touch on themes that are common across many philosophies and religions: harm, fairness, duty, rights, distribution, and liberty. We will focus on cases where there is not a clear "win-win" outcome. You don't need to read a book to tell you to take advantage of win-win situations. Rather, the key to leadership is managing difficult tradeoffs among stakeholders, when different values guide you in different ways. This is sometimes frustrating for managers since there isn't a clear answer or model they can apply as in finance or accounting. However, the reason why good leadership is so important, and so rare, is precisely because skilled leaders can grapple with ambiguous and uncertain situations.

Some people claim it's only important to study descriptive ethics or normative ethics in isolation, and see little value in the other approach. For example, in their book *Blind Spots*, psychologists Max Bazerman and Ann Tenbrunsel write: "Being taught which ethical judgment you should make is unlikely to improve your ethicality. By contrast, the lens of behavioral ethics should prove useful for those who wish to be more ethical human beings but whose judgments don't always live up to their ideals and expectations."[7] Similarly, in *The Righteous Mind*, psychologist Jonathan Haidt says: "The worship of reason, which is sometimes found in philosophical and scientific circles, is a delusion. It is an example of faith in something that does not exist."[8]

We reject this view if the goal is to be a well-rounded, thoughtful leader. Descriptive and normative ethics work together and reinforce one another in important ways. Without a core set of values from normative ethics, it is impossible to have a coherent and consistent framework to make tough decisions. And without an understanding of descriptive ethics, it is difficult to act on your values. Effective leaders both understand the right course of action that is consistent with their values, and the pitfalls and constraints of human psychology.

Throughout this book, we will also draw on a third field: political economy. This is the study of institutions, or an understanding of how businesses fit within society at large. A simplistic view of this relationship is the shareholder value model, which dominated business education in the 1970s and 1980s. In that view, the government acts on behalf of citizens to set the "rules of the game," and each company operates within these rules to achieve a single objective: maximizing long-run profits for its shareholders.

Over the years, this view has become increasingly untenable. Big business used to be a highly respected institution both in the United States and around the globe, but numerous ethical lapses, as well as instances of outright lawbreaking, have undermined this trust. A few prominent examples include Enron's accounting scandal, Theranos's fake blood testing technology, Purdue Pharma's pushing of addictive opioids, Volkswagen's manipulation of emissions testing, and the adverse effects of social media platforms such as Facebook and Twitter on democratic institutions. The 2008 financial crisis greatly decreased trust in business elites and contributed to populist revolts across the globe.

Hence, it is important for individual leaders to understand the broader political and social environment of business. Firms are no longer expected just to serve their shareholders, but also to be accountable to other stakeholders, including employees, customers, suppliers, citizens, civil society, and the media. Moreover, the "rules of the game" are not set in stone, but rather are determined by governments that are responsive to a variety of different constituencies, including voters, activists, and firms themselves. Participating in this process in a way that is both principled and effective requires a sophisticated understanding of societal values and institutions.

TYPES OF DILEMMAS

In teaching our class at Stanford, we have found that it is useful to discuss situations where *everyone agrees* on what is the right or wrong thing to do, as well as situations where people can *reasonably disagree*. Both types of situations are important for values-based leadership.

There are some courses of action that are clearly wrong. Pretty much everyone agrees that it's not acceptable to engage in sexual harassment, defraud shareholders, use racially discriminatory business practices, or sell extremely unsafe products to unsuspecting consumers. But even in situations where everyone agrees on the right thing to do, some individuals and organizations engage in behavior that is known to be wrong. In this book we will explain why that happens. A key takeaway is that unethical behavior is often not due to the malice of evil people, although that is certainly sometimes a factor. Rather, as we will discover, numerous psychological biases and phenomena can lead ordinarily good people to engage in unethical behavior. We will also discuss practical ways for leaders to rectify courses of action that are clearly wrong.

In other situations, well-intentioned people can reasonably disagree, because they come to the table with different sets of values. Delving into these issues is also important for a values-based leader. Critically analyzing controversial business decisions allows us to clarify our own values, understand others' perspectives, learn how to persuade, and achieve compromise. Again, a core theme of this book is that people are not binary (good or evil). Rather, good people can legitimately come to different conclusions about the right thing to do.

HANDLING DISAGREEMENT

To get at values disagreements, the topics that we will cover include a lot of hot-button issues. That is intentional. Values-based leadership isn't just for easy situations; it also requires leading and engaging with people when things get contentious.

A key skill in doing this is to identify the nature of a disagreement, especially whether it is about facts or about values. In a heated discussion, people often try to make any sort of argument that will bolster their side, and get so caught up in the moment that they can't even tell whether they are disagreeing about facts or values. This is important to sort out, because disagreements about facts and values are fundamentally different.

Take, for example, the debate about raising the minimum wage. Economic theory states that increasing the floor on wages increases unemployment because employers won't be willing to hire as many workers. There are disagreements about how elastic this relationship is – that is, whether an increase in the minimum wage causes a large or small decrease in employment – but economists collect data all the time to help resolve these debates.

It is harder to resolve debates that are about differences in values. For example, if increasing the minimum wage benefits workers who have a job but hurts consumers, businesses, and those who cannot find employment, what should the government do? There is no obviously correct way to decide whose interests to prioritize. The answer depends on values.

Disagreements about values can be extremely difficult to resolve. As much as you might want to convince someone that their values are wrong and they should instead adopt your values, that's a pretty tough goal to achieve. (If you find it easy, we suggest that you set aside your business career and instead become an evangelist, whether for a religion, a political party, or a social cause. Also, and more seriously, this is one reason we don't try very hard to convince our students or you, the reader, to agree with our own personal strongly held values. Both of us would make pretty lousy evangelists.)

Realizing that a disagreement is about values should change the nature of the conversation. As a first step, you can try to understand the other person's core convictions, treat them with respect, and see the issue from their perspective. In doing so, you will likely be able to identify some commonalities and points of agreement. You may even be able to win them over to your side; not by getting them to change their values, but rather by showing that the course of action you want to take is actually consistent with their own values.

THE JOURNEY AHEAD

Here's a roadmap of where we are going. The next few chapters discuss descriptive ethics, or how people (including you, the reader, and us, the authors) actually make ethical decisions. The analysis starts inside the deep subconscious of the mind, then moves outward toward individual conscious processes, and then further outward into the social environment. In these chapters, we aim to convince you of three key psychological facts: People's moral decisions are powerfully influenced by their initial gut reactions (Chapter 2); self-deception and rationalizations can make it easier for people to behave in ways that violate the law, corporate policies, and their own principles (Chapter 3); and people's behavior is powerfully influenced by their social environment, including authority figures and perceived social norms (Chapter 4).

Our goal in this part of the book is not to criticize human beings for hypocrisy and moral failures. That might be fun, and even entertaining, but it has few practical implications. Rather, once we understand the psychological constraints of ethical decision-making, we can learn to design organizations in ways that address these constraints. Leadership is of course about motivation and inspiration. But an underrated aspect of being a good leader is designing a good set of institutions, rules, and incentives, which is a central theme of this book.

We then turn to normative ethics, or the set of values we should use to make decisions and decide whether a course of action is right or wrong. Our approach is not to tell you to believe in a particular set of normative principles. Rather, we aim to convince you that you, and others around you, routinely make arguments about consequences, motives, and fairness. Given this, it is important to have philosophical frameworks to clarify and apply your principles and then engage constructively with people whose principles differ from your own.

Chapter 5 analyzes how market incentives and government policies encourage or discourage companies to take into account the well-being of others. Chapter 6 focuses on a common claim made by business leaders: that they care about how their actions impact society, or, more colloquially, that they are "making the world a better place." To assess this claim, we lay out a framework for evaluating the overall societal consequences of a decision.

Chapter 7 focuses on perspective-taking and the idea that respecting another person's human dignity requires treating them as a rational being with their own goals and desires, rather than simply using them as a means to achieve our own goals. This has profound implications in a wide range of business contexts, ranging from advertising to deal making. Chapter 8 addresses issues of fairness and justice, both within companies and at a societal level.

In the final chapter, we synthesize the material on descriptive and normative ethics and ask you to think about three of the most important questions for your life and career. What are your core values? How will you live by them? And how will you lead with them? Of course, you probably had a pretty good sense of your core values before you picked up this book. However, we hope that as you read the book we will challenge your assumptions and intuitions and help you to clarify your values structure. Perhaps you will change some of your beliefs. Additionally, we hope to help you predict and be prepared to navigate situations where your core values will be threatened.

We look forward to taking this journey with you. If you've gotten this far, you probably agree with us that values are central to leadership, and that it is important to articulate one's core values, stick with them, and live them with passion and purpose.

TAKEAWAYS

At the end of each chapter, we will summarize a few key takeaways. As you return to this book throughout your career, these will serve as helpful guidelines.

1. Leadership is about core values, that is, beliefs and convictions about what is important in life.
2. Values are inter-subjective: People hold different values but values are commonly shared by groups.

3. Effective leaders not only know their own values but can manage the diversity of values within their organizations.

4. To be an effective leader, one must understand both how people make ethical decisions (descriptive ethics) and what makes a decision ethical or unethical (normative ethics). Only by combining both approaches can we be prepared to act on our core values in difficult situations.

5. Normal people sometimes do unethical things, often not because they are bad people, but because of psychological constraints and badly designed institutions.

6. Effective leaders structure the rules in their organizations to induce people to act on their values.

7. In some situations, well-meaning people can legitimately disagree on the ethical course of action, because they prioritize different values.

SUGGESTIONS FOR FURTHER READING

At the end of each chapter, we will recommend some additional reading if you want to dive deeper into some of the topics. If you are interested in watching Steve Jobs's full speech, it is available on YouTube: www.youtube.com/watch?v=keCwRdbwNQY. For more details on anthropological and evolutionary accounts of values as mechanisms for human cooperation, two excellent books are Yuval Noah Harari's *Sapiens: A Brief History of Humankind* and Joshua Greene's *Moral Tribes: Emotion, Reason, and the Gap Between Us and Them*.

REFLECTIVE EXERCISES

Finally, before moving onto the next chapter, we will raise some questions for reflection. Feel free to use these questions in ways that are helpful to you. You can jot down your responses in a journal. You can discuss them with colleagues, friends, mentors, mentees, and loved ones. Or you can just reflect privately.

1. Think about a product or service you love, or a company or leader you admire. What are the core values of the company or leader?

2. As a first cut (before reading the rest of this book), jot down what you consider to be your core values in life and as a leader of your

organization. Do you hold these values privately? Do you share them with others?

3. Think about a controversial issue in politics, business, or some other domain. Why do you think people disagree over this issue? What core values are at stake, and how do they divide people?

2

Follow Your Gut?

In the early 1900s, an average of 1,528 Americans died from smallpox each year. A few decades later, that number was zero. In the early 1950s, there were 16,316 cases of polio each year, with a mortality rate of over 10 percent. By the 1980s, the number of cases was in the single digits. For measles, the numbers dropped from 508,282 cases and 432 deaths per year in the 1950s and 1960s to fewer than 100 cases and zero deaths per year in the 1990s.[1]

Decreases in these illnesses were not limited to the United States. Globally, the number of annual deaths from measles fell from one million in the mid-1980s to around 100,000 in the mid-2010s. And smallpox, which killed hundreds of millions of people during the twentieth century – more than the combined toll of World Wars I and II – was completely eradicated throughout the world.

This seems like a miracle, but it's easy to explain: It's a direct result of vaccines, which have dramatically reduced the number of infections and deaths from many previously common diseases. Vaccines are one of the greatest human inventions, a fact underscored by the arrival of the coronavirus pandemic in 2020, when many realized what it was like to be at the mercy of a novel disease.

Given this, you might expect that people would jump at the possibility to get themselves and their children vaccinated. Indeed, a substantial majority of children in the United States are vaccinated on the schedule recommended by scientists, doctors, and the government.

But an increasing number aren't. In the mid-2010s, 1.3 percent of two-year-olds hadn't received *any* vaccines and only 69 percent had received the full set of vaccines. In part, this was because of missed medical appointments, especially for families without health insurance. But it was also partially due to parents choosing to avoid or delay vaccinations. Skipping or delaying vaccines is dangerous, both for an individual child and for others in society who have allergies or health conditions that prevent them from getting vaccinated. In recent years, outbreaks of preventable diseases, especially measles and whooping cough, have returned to the United States. According to Gallup, the number of Americans who say it is extremely or very important for parents to get their children vaccinated fell from 94 percent in 2001 to 84 percent in 2015. In 2019, 16 percent of Americans with children under the age of 18 said they think vaccines are more dangerous than the diseases they are designed to prevent.[2]

A major contributor to these trends is the anti-vaccine or "antivax" movement, which claims that vaccines are unnecessary and harmful. An especially frightening claim – that the chemicals in vaccines cause autism – originated in a 1998 study by Andrew Wakefield in *Lancet*, one of the leading medical journals in the world. The study was later found to be deeply flawed; the article was retracted, and Wakefield lost his medical license. Many subsequent studies have found no evidence that vaccines cause autism. But the claim persists, and has been repeated by numerous celebrities, including Robert De Niro, Jenny McCarthy, and Bill Maher. In the 2019 Gallup survey, 15 percent of parents of young children said that vaccines cause autism, 42 percent said they don't, and 43 percent were unsure.

This argument has caught on in communities where organic food, yoga, and herbal remedies are popular. For example, in some wealthy, highly educated, liberal parts of Los Angeles, vaccination rates were as low as South Sudan's and there were multiple outbreaks of diseases like whooping cough.[3]

In other communities, different fears come to the fore. Some social conservatives object to Gardasil, a vaccine against the human papillomavirus (HPV), a sexually transmitted disease that causes genital warts and cervical cancer. This view was articulated by Bridget Maher, a spokeswoman for the influential Christian conservative group, the Family Research Council, who said that "[g]iving the HPV vaccine to young women could be potentially harmful because they may see it as a license to engage in premarital sex."[4]

Another set of fears arose in Jewish and Muslim communities, regarding vaccines whose ingredients include gelatin derived from pigs. Leading rabbis have concluded that Jewish dietary laws do not apply to non-oral products and, even if they did, the principle of saving lives takes precedence over other tenets of Jewish law. International Islamic legal scholars have concluded that the process of turning pig parts into gelatin for medical applications transforms a substance that is originally impure into another substance that is pure and lawful.

Antivax activists see things differently. A cartoon in a pamphlet distributed to Orthodox Jews in Brooklyn contrasted an image of two happy unvaccinated children against a cartoon of a massive syringe labeled "DTaP vaccine" with contents labeled as "Pig and monkey cells" along with "Mercury," "Undetected viruses," "Acetone," "Formaldehyde," "Antifreeze," "Peanut Oil," and "Aborted Fetal Tissue." In Indonesia, the Ulema Council (the country's top Islamic authority) went against international Islamic legal scholars and ruled that a measles–rubella vaccine was proscribed as haram, because it contained some ingredients derived from pigs. Vaccination rates subsequently plummeted, despite the fact that the council explicitly said that, due to the dangers of not being vaccinated, the current version could be used until an acceptable halal variant was developed.[5]

At this point, you may have a guess about the lesson that we're driving at in this story. Given that we're professors and scholars, you might expect us to argue that people should rely on research by reputable scientific experts rather than their own gut intuitions or claims made by celebrities. And you'd be correct that we're very much in favor of facts and careful research. But that's not our point.

Our point, which may surprise you, is that most people who are skeptical or opposed to vaccines are not crazy. Rather, *the gut intuitions that drive their views are fundamentally normal*.

Antivaxers are flat-out wrong about the risks and rewards of vaccines, and their behavior is a serious threat to public health. But their trust in regular people's accounts of their experiences, along with their belief in urban legends and rumors rather than scientific studies, has deep commonalities with the ways that most people assess evidence. Their instinct to cast blame on companies that produce vaccines is extreme, but fundamentally similar to the approach taken by many other people. Their moral intuitions – whether about avoiding impurities (chemicals, sex, or pork) and harms (alleged side effects of vaccines), or about standing up for their individual liberty and against the government – draw on the same foundations that most people use when making gut-level moral assessments of right and wrong. And the fact that their instinctive reactions strongly influence their assessment of arguments and evidence is not at all strange. In fact, it's something we all do.[6]

There has been a lot of debate recently about whether people should carefully reason through each decision or instead rely on gut instincts to avoid "analysis paralysis." An immensely popular book by Malcolm Gladwell, *Blink: The Power of Thinking without Thinking*, came down on the side of gut instinct. Many scholars deeply disagreed with Gladwell's approach and conclusions.[7]

We bring a novel perspective to this debate: Both sides of the argument are missing the point. We reject the premise of the question, because both modes of decision-making – careful analysis and gut-level reactions – are inherent parts of all human beings. Saying that we shouldn't use our gut is like saying we shouldn't breathe. The key is getting our gut and our brains in sync so they can talk to each other in a productive fashion.

Over the course of this chapter, we will develop these points, drawing on cutting-edge research from the field of moral psychology. But first we're going to set the stage with some background about how human thought processes operate.

WE'RE NOT *THE THINKER*

Rodin's *The Thinker* sits, leaning forward, with his head resting on his hand. Initially, he was Dante, perched atop Rodin's monumental sculpture *The Gates of Hell*. Later, Rodin cast *The Thinker* alone, as a massive freestanding sculpture (see Figure 2.1[8]). In that iconic version, it's not clear who he is or what he is pondering. But he's definitely concentrating deeply. The muscles of his powerful body are not about to jump into action; rather, they are committed to focusing his mind on the mental task at hand.

In many ways, *The Thinker* epitomizes what universities are all about, which is probably why castings of it are proudly displayed at several schools around the world. At Stanford, he used to sit outside the entrance to a library, as if to tell students, silently but powerfully, "*This* is what you do here."

Universities place enormous value on careful, painstaking thought. The logic of an argument must be valid. The data behind an empirical claim must be sound. The craftsmanship of a sonata or short story must be impeccable. It isn't enough to just assert something – "the earth is flat" or "the sun revolves around the earth." You have to prove it is true.

Cognitive psychologists have a phrase for the type of cogitation embodied by *The Thinker*. They call it *System 2*. System 2 is slow. It requires conscious effort. It is careful and deliberate.

FIGURE 2.1. *The Thinker*

But, as the name "System 2" suggests, there's another type of cognition: one that is much more common, and in important ways more
fundamental. It's called (unsurprisingly) *System 1*. System 1 is fast. So
fast, in fact, that it operates with little or no effort. It is neither careful nor
deliberate – we have so little control over it that we find it difficult to turn
off. System 1 is what you're using to translate the shapes on this page into
meaningful language.[9]

System 1 is what you use to solve an equation like $3 + 3 = \_\_$. System
2 is what you use to solve an equation like $x^2 + 10x-299 = 0$.

When you walk through your neighborhood to visit a friend, System
1 gets you there. When you look at a map to navigate around a strange
city, you use System 2.

As these examples suggest, System 1 is incredibly useful, because it
enables us to handle routine tasks. It would be unbelievably difficult – in
fact, impossible – to get through the day if we had to devote focused
cognitive effort to everything we do.

How about our judgment and decision-making? Are they System 1 or
System 2? The answer is a bit of each, but much more System 1 than you
might expect. In one of the most influential papers in the social sciences,
psychologists Daniel Kahneman and Amos Tversky studied several *heuristics*, or cognitive shortcuts, that people use when assessing evidence and

making decisions. Heuristics are generally useful, and lead to pretty reasonable conclusions most of the time, but sometimes they lead to substantial errors in judgment.[10]

Kahneman and Tversky's work on heuristics and their subsequent theoretical work on decision-making under uncertainty posed a fundamental challenge to economic theory, which is mainly based on models of rational, optimizing System 2 decision-makers. The challenge was so successful that Kahneman won the 2002 Nobel Prize in Economics. (Tversky would have received it along with him, but had died of pancreatic cancer in 1996.)

One of the most well-established heuristics is the *availability heuristic*.[11] Suppose we ask you to estimate how many seven-letter English-language words end in "-ing." How would you go about answering that question? A natural way is by thinking of examples of such words. And doing that is easy. In fact, in writing this paragraph we're giving you some hints: "answering," "thinking," "doing," "writing," and "giving." Not all of these have seven letters, but you probably realized that "-ing" can be tacked on to any verb – running, jumping, talking, and countless others – so you probably came up with a pretty high estimate of the number of seven-letter words that end in "-ing."

But what if we had instead asked you to estimate how many seven-letter English-language words have "n" as their sixth letter? For this question, it's much harder to think of examples, unless you happen to stumble upon the trick that all words ending in "-ing" have "n" as their penultimate letter. So you probably would come up with a lower estimate, despite the fact that there are more seven-letter words with n as their sixth letter than seven-letter words ending in "-ing."[12]

What's going on here is an example of the availability heuristic: judging the frequency or probability of an event by seeing how easily instances of it can be brought to mind. This heuristic has been demonstrated in a large number of experiments. It also comes into play in everyday life. If you get into an argument with your spouse or roommate about who does more of the housework, you can easily think of times you did the dishes, took out the trash, or vacuumed, but it's much harder to think of times they scrubbed the sink, did the laundry, or weeded the garden, especially if you weren't even present when they did those things. The availability heuristic can lead each person to unintentionally underestimate and undervalue the other's contributions.

The availability heuristic may also explain some people's fears that vaccines cause autism. A good scientific way to assess this causal relationship is to compare rates of autism among vaccinated children against rates of autism in a similar population of unvaccinated children. That's what *The Thinker* would do (and he likely would put in a ton of effort to figure out how to ensure that the two populations being compared in the study were similar).

In contrast, a person who uses the availability heuristic simply thinks of examples of children who were vaccinated and have autism. These may come from their personal experience, stories from friends, or news on the Internet. Given that most children get vaccines, and antivax activists are quite active on social media, it's easy to think of stories. As an example of this way of thinking, in 2014 Donald Trump, who at the time was mainly known as a reality TV star, tweeted, "Healthy young child goes to doctor, gets pumped with massive shot of many vaccines, doesn't feel good and changes – AUTISM. Many such cases!"[13] To assess the risks from vaccines this way is incorrect, but it's completely normal.

If you're interested in learning more about System 1 and System 2, heuristics, and cognitive psychology more generally, we strongly recommend that you read Kahneman's excellent book *Thinking Fast and Slow*. But now we're going to head in a different direction, examining how these insights about human cognition apply not just to judgments about data but also to judgments about right and wrong.

MORAL INTUITIONS AND MORAL HEURISTICS

If you were to ask *The Thinker* about a moral issue, how would he approach it? He'd presumably make sure to get all the relevant facts and data. He'd then carefully work through how the issue connects to his core values. Surely his approach would be logical and systematic. If the issue was particularly complicated, he might even get off his pedestal and walk over to the library, so that he could benefit from centuries of wisdom from philosophers and religious scholars.

Like *The Thinker*, you've done this sort of analysis of right and wrong, whether in a college class, a debate tournament, a late-night conversation with friends, or with members of your religious community. It's something we're all capable of, using our System 2.

But System 2 is not the starting point for how we make moral judgments. Rather, System 1 moves first, providing our *moral intuitions*, which are our immediate reactions that something is morally right or morally wrong. These intuitions are quick, almost effortless, and sometimes can be hard to describe, other than saying "I just feel in my gut that ... ." Moral intuitions are also often accompanied by emotion, whether joy, hope, gratitude, anger, fear, shame, sadness, disgust, or righteous condemnation.

This isn't necessarily a problem. It would be pretty bad if human beings always had to carefully think through every moral decision, and couldn't rely on immediate emotional reactions. The problem, though, is that it's hard to get unstuck from our original System 1 position. System 2 reasoning, when used at all, is often employed to justify and rationalize the initial System 1 response. All of the skills of argumentation and analysis that we use as leaders often are in service of our gut. And much of moral philosophy could be described as people writing long books that attempt to systematize and justify System 1 responses using System 2 reasoning.

As with questions about facts and data, our moral judgments are affected by the way our minds work. We don't just use heuristics for questions about the number of words ending in "-ing" or the risks of vaccines. We also use them for questions about right and wrong. Thus, moral reasoning is just like most other types of reasoning.

When we try to make sense of the world, we often break things into categories, and moral reasoning is no exception. One example of a moral heuristic people use when evaluating a conflict is to divide things up into *moral agents* and *moral patients* so that we can answer questions like "Who can do wrong?" and "Who can be wronged?" Ethicists use the term *moral agent* to refer to someone who is capable of thinking about and making moral judgments and therefore can be held responsible for their actions. A *moral patient*, on the other hand, is someone who is capable of feeling harm and thus can have right or wrong done to them. If someone is a moral patient, then others have a responsibility to take them into consideration. These differences don't just matter for ethicists – they also matter for regular people, because our moral assessment of an action often depends on who is doing it and who is having it done to them.[14] People frequently have a construction akin to the matrix in Table 2.1 in their heads.

At first glance, it may seem that everyone is both a moral agent and a moral patient (see upper-left box of Table 2.1). Think of one of your friends or coworkers: They surely can do right and wrong, and surely can have right and wrong done to them.

But what about small children? Are they morally responsible for their actions? If a two-year-old snatches a cookie away from another child and eats it, you may react negatively and you might even scold them. But you

TABLE 2.1. *Moral agents and patients*

	Can Be a Moral Patient	Cannot Be a Moral Patient
Can Be a Moral Agent	Adults, Teenagers	Corporations, Cyborgs
Cannot Be a Moral Agent	Small Children, Animals	Rocks, Inanimate Objects

probably don't think there is anything seriously morally wrong about their behavior.

How about dogs? If a dog runs up to you and bites you on the arm, you will be upset. You might yell "bad dog!" and you might mean it. But you'd be much more upset if your coworker ran up to you and bit you on the arm – that's the behavior of a sociopath.

In contrast to adults, we don't hold small children and dogs morally responsible for their actions. They aren't moral agents. But they surely *are* moral patients. To see this, just think about your instinctive reaction if you see a child or dog being mistreated.

Inanimate objects like rocks and boulders are neither agents nor patients. Nobody would call a rock a victim if someone kicked it. And nobody would charge a boulder for murder if it fell on a hiker.

OK, so far we've talked about adults, children, dogs, and boulders as moral agents and patients. How about companies? Companies differ from these other examples in many ways, including that they are, in the arc of human history, a rather new phenomenon.

Like many aspects of our human cognitive apparatus, our instinctive sense of who has moral responsibilities, and to whom they have those responsibilities, evolved with our species. For almost all of our evolutionary history, our ancestors lived in small groups, so our cognitive apparatus only had to deal with situations that were important in those small groups. At the very last evolutionary moment – the past few thousand years – we have developed civilizations that feature all sorts of organizational structures completely unlike anything encountered by our hunter-gatherer ancestors.

So it's not obvious what our minds, which evolved in a very different setting, would make of all of this modern complexity. How do we think about a government? A corporation? Are they moral agents? Are they moral patients? Both? Neither?

According to management scholars Tage Rai and Daniel Diermeier, most people see corporations as being moral agents.[15] In other words, even though corporations are massive organizations, we see them as being capable of formulating intent and knowing right from wrong. This means they can be villains – not just an individual executive but rather the corporation itself. As stated in a 2020 *Slate.com* article discussing a survey about the most evil tech companies, "We don't mean evil in the mustache-twirling, burn-the-world-from-a-secret-lair sense ... but rather in the way Googlers once swore to avoid mission drift, respect their users, and spurn short-term profiteering, even though the company now regularly faces scandals in which it has violated its users' or workers' trust."[16]

On the flip side, if companies are moral agents, capable of doing right and wrong, this also means they can be heroes. Sometimes they can even transform themselves from villains to heroes. For example, Walmart, which has come under intense criticism for paying low wages and decimating local businesses, has also received widespread praise for how it handles hurricanes. In the days leading up to landfall of a storm, the company's logistical prowess enables it to rapidly distribute crucial supplies to its stores, and the company's senior executives are very focused on making sure that things run as smoothly as possible. In the horrific aftermath of Hurricane Katrina in 2005, Walmart donated a substantial amount of goods and services, but just as important was the simple fact that Walmart was skilled at getting goods to people who desperately needed them. As described in a *Washington Post* article, "While state and federal officials have come under harsh criticism for their handling of the storm's aftermath, Walmart is being held up as a model for logistical efficiency and nimble disaster planning, which have allowed it to quickly deliver staples such as water, fuel and toilet paper to thousands of evacuees."[17]

So, in the eyes of most people, companies are moral agents, who can think, and thus can do right and wrong. But are they moral patients? Can they be the victims of wrongdoing? Rai and Diermeier show that most people don't see things that way. Rather, they typically see companies as being incapable of feeling and thus unworthy of sympathy. In this way, they are similar to Arnold Schwarzenegger's cyborg character (the T-800) in *The Terminator* movies. Sometimes a villain, sometimes a hero, but never a victim.

This creates a fundamental asymmetry in how we see interactions between individuals and companies. Suppose an HMO or insurance company mistakenly sends a coworker of yours a bill saying they owe the company a $200 copayment for a doctor's visit that actually should be fully covered by their insurance plan. Your coworker would be outraged, and so would you, especially if it was difficult to get the company to correct the bill. You might even suspect that the company intentionally set up a billing system that was prone to making errors in its favor. But if the roles were reversed, and it was your coworker who failed to pay money they owed the company, you probably wouldn't be very mad at them, even if they ignored the company's first couple of attempts to get them to pay. You might even root for them to get off without paying. And you almost certainly wouldn't feel any sympathy for an HMO or insurance company. Numerous experiments by management scholars Arthur Jago and Jeffrey Pfeffer show that people punish corporations much more than individuals, even when they are committing the same transgressions: engaging in deception, reneging on contracts, harming consumers, or polluting the environment.[18]

This dynamic also comes into play in the battle over vaccines. Pharmaceutical companies are widely perceived as being selfish and unconcerned about people's well-being. So if they try to speed up the approval process for a vaccine or if they lobby the government to mandate vaccines, they fit neatly into a narrative about greedy corporate villains. If a company were to get caught telling blatant lies about its vaccines, there would be hell to pay. And if a vaccine ended up being unsafe or inadvertently causing deaths, the company would be badly punished in the court of public opinion.

In contrast, when antivax activists spread all sorts of misinformation, fabrications, and conspiracy theories, they don't come under the same level of moral scrutiny. They are typically criticized as being crazy rather than evil. And when they are criticized on moral grounds, the criticism is on behalf of regular people, especially children, who suffer from illness as a result of reduced vaccination levels. Nobody feels sympathy for the pharmaceutical companies whose products are being badmouthed (except, possibly, employees of those companies).

FOUNDATIONS OF MORAL INTUITIONS

At this point, we have hopefully convinced you that System 1 powerfully shapes how people think about moral questions, whether about their own lives, companies' behavior, or broad societal issues. While interesting, this by itself does not provide strategic guidance for leadership. However, scholars also have a good sense of how moral intuitions are structured, which allows us to predict and manage stakeholder responses. We'll now delve more deeply into the structure of moral intuitions.

In his book *The Righteous Mind*, the psychologist Jonathan Haidt describes five senses that serve as foundations of moral intuition: preventing *harm*, ensuring *fairness*, loyalty to one's *ingroup*, respect for *authority*, and maintaining *purity*.[19]

Haidt and his research collaborators Jesse Graham and Brian Nosek asked a large number of people how much they agree with several statements that embody each of the five moral senses.[20] Here are two examples for each foundation.

- If I saw a mother slapping her child, I would be outraged. (harm)
- Compassion for those who are suffering is the most crucial virtue. (harm)
- If a friend wanted to cut in with me on a long line, I would feel uncomfortable because it wouldn't be fair to those behind me. (fairness)
- Justice, fairness, and equality are the most important requirements for a society. (fairness)
- When it comes to close friendships and romantic relationships, it is OK for people to seek out members of their own ethnic or religious group. (ingroup)
- The government should strive to improve the well-being of people in our nation, even if it sometimes happens at the expense of people in other nations. (ingroup)
- If I were a soldier and disagreed with my commanding officer's orders, I would obey anyway because that is my duty. (authority)
- Respect for authority is something all children need to learn. (authority)
- I would call some acts wrong on the grounds that they are unnatural or disgusting. (purity)
- The government should try to help people live virtuously and avoid sin. (purity)

People's reactions to statements that draw on the five moral foundations exhibit interesting patterns. Everyone places at least *some* value on each of the foundations, though the specific ways we value the foundation vary from person to person. For example, some people are concerned about harm to animals, but others are not. Similarly, people disagree about what level of physical punishment of a child is harmful, but everyone has some level beyond which they would consider corporal punishment unacceptable.

The relative emphasis that people put on the five foundations also varies across cultures. Western moral philosophy places great weight on harm and fairness, which are values designed to protect the *individual*. In many non-Western societies (and in less-cosmopolitan areas of Western societies), people care more about the social units larger than the individual (e.g., communities, villages, and nations) and therefore place weight on the other three moral senses: ingroup, authority, and purity.

Haidt claims that these five moral foundations have an evolutionary basis. For example, the instinct to view harm as immoral is core to mammals' need to care for their young. In early tribal societies, the stability of the group was based on people respecting the community as well as authority figures. In hunter-gatherer societies, people had to constantly be on the lookout for pestilence and poisonous foods, so they developed an instinctive disgust for impurities. We won't go so far as to say that moral intuitions are completely based on genetics or human evolution. Most likely, these moral senses are a product of both evolution and cultural transmission, which explains why there are cultural differences in morality across societies.

Even within societies, there is variation between people with different political leanings. The ways a moral sense is expressed often differ between liberals and conservatives. For example, liberals in the United States often conceive of fairness in terms of "equality," (i.e., were people treated equally?) whereas conservatives conceive of it in terms of "proportionality" (i.e., did people get what they deserve?). We'll return to these differences in Chapter 8 when we discuss fairness and justice.

The overall weight that people place on the different moral senses is also related to their political leanings. In the United States, liberals are especially attuned to harm and fairness, and place a lower value on ingroup, authority, and purity. People towards the conservative end of the spectrum care a bit less about harm and fairness and they care a lot more about ingroup, authority, and purity.

You may wonder whether what's going on here is that some of the survey questions used by Haidt and his coauthors sound like they're about public policy, in which case the survey might just be picking up people's political identities. But the same pattern shows up in questions that, on their face, have nothing to do with politics. For example, consider the following set of questions: How much would I need to pay you to ... ?

- Stick a pin into the palm of a child you don't know. (harm)
- Say no to a friend's request to help you move into a new apartment, after they'd helped you move the month before. (fairness)
- Publicly bet against your favorite sports team. (ingroup)

- Slap your father in the face (with his permission) as part of a comedy skit. (authority)
- Get a blood transfusion of 1 pint of disease-free, compatible blood from a convicted child molester. (purity)

Some of these questions are pretty wacky, and they're definitely not about politics or public policy. But they nonetheless seem to tap into moral intuitions that are correlated with people's political leanings. People from across the political spectrum say they'd need to be paid a substantial amount of money to violate harm and fairness. Conservatives also are reluctant to violate ingroup, authority, and purity. For instance, conservatives require more money than liberals to "burn your country's flag in private" (ingroup) and "sign a piece of paper that says 'I hereby sell my soul, after my death, to whoever has this piece of paper'" (purity). To liberals, in contrast, these transgressions aren't as big a deal, because to them a flag is just a piece of cloth, and a "soul certificate" is just a piece of paper. They don't share conservatives' System 1 reactions to these transgressions.

Conflicts between the moral foundations play a crucial role in many values-based disagreements, including the dispute over vaccines. People who advocate for vaccines are motivated by concerns about harm (preventing disease and death) and fairness (especially to people with compromised immune systems, who must rely on others getting vaccinated to prevent disease outbreaks).

Antivax advocates are also motivated by harm (fears of autism and adverse reactions). Many of them have strong moral intuitions about purity, though there is variation in what impurities they find problematic: unnatural chemicals and toxins for California liberals, premarital sex for Christian conservatives, and ingredients derived from pigs for Jews and Muslims.

The vaccine controversy also ties in to a sixth moral foundation that Haidt has developed in his more recent research: *liberty* from oppression.[21] This clearly is a strong instinctive motivation for conservatives and libertarians who feel that government vaccine requirements are a coercive infringement on their individual rights. For example, Arizona State Representative Kelly Townsend posted on Facebook: "Our country is sovereign, our State is sovereign, our family is sovereign, our God is sovereign and the most holy and sacred last frontier of sovereignty is our own body ... The idea that we force someone to give up their liberty for the sake of the collective is not based on American values but rather,

Communist."[22] For some people, the government mandating vaccines for schoolchildren is akin to the government poking you with a sharp object without your consent.

Looking ahead a bit, we'll revisit the topic of liberty (Chapter 8), as well as harm (Chapter 6), and fairness (Chapter 8). In those chapters we will explore philosophical arguments that put an analytical structure on these moral senses.

STRATEGIES FOR DECISION-MAKING AND LEADERSHIP

Based on the psychology research that we've presented in this chapter, it might be tempting to conclude that the key to effective decision-making is using System 2 rather than System 1. But that's not what we're going to recommend. There are two key reasons for this.

First, System 1 has a sneaky but powerful ability to infiltrate and influence people's System 2 reasoning. Quite often, our gut reactions drive our analytical thinking, so that when we do a quantitative or strategic analysis we're merely justifying our initial (System 1) decision. This is true whether the analysis is focused on facts and data or values and moral reasoning. As an example, read the story below. As you read, try to set aside your System 1 gut reaction and just analyze the situation like *The Thinker*, using only System 2.

A family's dog, Scooter, was killed by a car in front of their house. Although saddened, the family wanted to celebrate the happy times they had with Scooter. They had been planning to have steak for dinner, but they remembered they'd heard that dog meat was delicious. So they cleaned and prepared the body, barbequed it on the grill, and ate it for dinner. Is this wrong?

This is a variant of a story used by Jonathan Haidt to demonstrate a phenomenon he calls "moral dumbfounding." Many people have an immediate gut instinct that the family's behavior was deviant, and even abhorrent. But it's hard to put a finger on exactly why. It's not like the family killed Scooter or treated him badly while he was alive. Eating Scooter rather than steak was surely better for the planet, because beef production creates a lot of greenhouse gasses. It also may have saved some cow's life. Yet, especially for people who come from cultures where pet dogs are practically part of the family, the story is deeply disturbing, and many will search long and hard for a rational analysis that lines up with their gut instincts.

Many of these gut reactions differ across cultures. If you presented a version of this vignette in parts of India, with a family eating a cow, you might observe a similar reaction. What animals are considered sacred varies across cultures; these System 1 responses have been ingrained within people via generations of cultural transmission.

Similarly, you can probably think of times when you've been involved in heated disputes with a friend, spouse, or coworker, who concocted all sorts of logical arguments and evidence to buttress their position. Maybe, being honest, you recognize times when you've done the same thing yourself. (Each of the authors can think of times that we've done it.)

So, all in all, we think it's a fool's errand to simply decide to be *The Thinker* and use our reason to override gut intuitions.

The second reason we don't advise you to simply rely on System 2 is that System 1 is quite useful. As we've already noted, it does a pretty good job of handling all sorts of routine decisions, both about facts and about values.

It's also useful in extraordinary circumstances. A study of people who were awarded the Carnegie Hero Medal for risking their lives to save other people, including complete strangers, found that they acted on impulse, following their gut intuitions about the right thing to do. Similarly, non-Jews who rescued Jews from the Nazis were often unable to provide any System 2 explanation for why they behaved so differently from others around them. According to Mordecai Paldiel of the Yad Vashem Holocaust Remembrance Center, "Explanations such as: 'anybody would have done what I did,' seem to point to a course of action done without premeditation, almost instinctively. It may be that the trauma of the senselessness of the situation pushed them to a primal and precognitive level in their response to it."[23]

So you can't, and shouldn't, try to stamp out your System 1 instincts. But what can you do about situations where your System 1 might be mistaken but you're unsure? Those can and do arise, and it's important to have a plan to deal with them.

Our advice is that you shouldn't try to go it alone as a leader, but rather rely on your *organization* and those around you to help you make better decisions. Organizations are good at decomposing problems into specific questions. Experts on those questions can then provide informed input to the leaders who are ultimately responsible for making a decision.

Here are a few examples of how moral intuitions pop up in the business world and how being attuned to intuitions can improve strategic leadership.

Intel and Conflict Minerals

As COO of Intel, Brian Krzanich was responsible for overseeing a complicated supply chain that transformed minerals and other raw materials into masterfully fabricated, state-of-the-art microprocessors.

In 2009, Intel received a letter from an activist group, the Enough Project, saying that some of the minerals used in the company's products came from warlord-controlled mines in the Democratic Republic of Congo (DRC). According to many experts, revenue from tin, tungsten, tantalum, and gold (also known as "conflict minerals") helped warlords finance a brutal, decades-long conflict, which had led to millions of deaths, hundreds of thousands of rapes, and an ongoing humanitarian disaster.[24]

According to Krzanich, upon hearing about this: "I had an immediate and visceral reaction. If we were contributing to human rights issues, we needed to figure out how not to contribute to that ... The initial thought was just to stop sourcing from the region altogether, thus avoiding conflict minerals from dubious sources."

Krzanich's initial System 1 reaction was very much in line with the purity moral foundation – he was proud of his company's products and wanted to ensure that they were not morally contaminated by minerals that funded atrocities. It would have been fairly straightforward for Intel to source raw materials from other regions – for example, by using tin from Indonesia and tantalum from Brazil and Australia.

However, members of Krzanich's team who were experts on conflict minerals pointed out that if companies stopped sourcing from the DRC, this would harm the livelihoods of people struggling to get by in one of the world's poorest countries. Although there were many warlord-controlled mines in the DRC, there were also many legitimate mines. In a country where most people earn less than a dollar per day, miners who lost their jobs would have few other ways to make a living and support their families.

This argument, about the consequences of completely avoiding DRC-produced minerals is a more analytical, System 2, way of thinking about the problem. But, importantly, it's also anchored in gut intuitions, specifically the moral foundation of harm (to miners who would lose their jobs).

Krzanich found this argument compelling. So instead of completely avoiding minerals from the DRC, Intel set up a team of several executives to work on the issue, including Carolyn Duran (an engineer and supply chain expert) and Gary Niekerk (Intel's director of corporate citizenship).

For several years, Intel worked with activist groups and other electronics companies to develop a certification system for minerals from legitimate mines within the DRC. By 2014, Intel was able to certify that all of its microprocessors were conflict free, while sourcing minerals in a way that contributed to the DRC economy. This program became a point of pride for many Intel employees and managers, who saw it as a reflection of their company's values and skill at solving difficult problems.

Amazon vs. Christian Smalls

As the coronavirus pandemic surged through the United States in late March 2020, cities and states implemented "shelter-in-place" rules and closed most businesses. This drove a dramatic increase in sales for online retailers like Amazon, which hired hundreds of thousands of new workers as it struggled to fulfill orders. The company had previously come under intense criticism for the demands that it placed on warehouse workers, and in the era of coronavirus, critics argued that the company placed its workers' lives in danger by failing to establish proper procedures for social distancing.

In New York City, which was the initial epicenter of the pandemic in the United States, an employee named Christian Smalls organized a lunchtime walkout at Amazon's Staten Island warehouse. As described by the *New York Times*, "They were calling simply for the building to be temporarily closed and more stringently sanitized and for workers to be paid during the hiatus as several had become sick." Amazon immediately fired Mr. Smalls, and the company later released a statement saying that he had failed to follow social distancing rules, and had come to work despite being told to stay home with pay after coming into contact with a fellow worker who had been diagnosed with COVID-19. The firing of Smalls quickly became a heated political issue, with the mayor and state attorney general calling for investigations, and presidential candidate Bernie Sanders tweeting that the company's actions were "absolutely immoral."[25]

Amazon's Senior VP of Global Communications and Senior VP of Global Operations quickly tweeted back at Sanders, using identical language saying that Mr. Smalls was at fault, because he "purposely violated social distancing rules, repeatedly."

The plan behind this coordinated attack on Mr. Smalls became public when *Vice News* obtained notes from a meeting of the company's top executives, including CEO Jeff Bezos. Written by General Counsel David

Zapolsky, the memo said: "We should spend the first part of our response strongly laying out the case for why the organizer's conduct was immoral, unacceptable, and arguably illegal, in detail, and only then follow with our usual talking points about worker safety." Zapolsky said that the company should "Make him the most interesting part of the story, and if possible make him the face of the entire union/organizing movement." And he further went on to argue that this approach was likely to succeed, because Smalls was "not smart, or articulate, and to the extent the press wants to focus on us versus him, we will be in a much stronger PR position than simply explaining for the umpteenth time how we're trying to protect workers."

Needless to say, Zapolsky's prediction about PR benefits turned out to be incorrect. By attacking Mr. Smalls, Amazon just made the story bigger. It played perfectly into the narrative of those who criticized the company for ruthlessly pursuing efficiency, without regard for the well-being of employees. And the fact that the attack was intentional and planned only made matters worse. Zapolsky quickly wrote an apology, saying that "I let my emotions draft my words and get the better of me."

One could debate endlessly whether Amazon was morally justified in firing Mr. Smalls, using criteria that we will discuss later in this book, including companies' responsibilities to shareholders and stakeholders (Chapter 5), the consequences of companies' actions (Chapter 6), perspective-taking (Chapter 7), and fairness and liberty (Chapter 8).

But even if you think Amazon did the right thing by firing Mr. Smalls, it's pretty clear that the company made a mistake in how it handled the situation. This mistake was not just the fact that the memo planning a PR campaign against Mr. Smalls was widely distributed and thus likely to leak. Rather, the company's entire approach to the situation was flawed. The company's leaders let their own System 1 reactions get the better of them and failed to realize that most people would have much more empathy for a warehouse worker whose health was at risk than for a gigantic company and its executives. Even a basic understanding of the moral agents vs. moral patients framework that we introduced earlier in this chapter would have been enough to make the company's leaders see that attacking an employee who had been exposed to the coronavirus while working at an Amazon warehouse was a very bad idea.

The Ethics of Pricing

Another business area where moral intuitions pop up is pricing. Companies often charge different prices to different consumers based on differences in their willingness or ability to pay for the same product. This is what economists call "price discrimination" and it's an effective way for companies to boost their profits. Sometimes people view price discrimination as ethical and sometimes they do not. For instance, many people would say it's totally fine for florists to raise prices on holidays such as Mother's Day and Valentine's Day, or for Uber and Lyft to charge more during busy times such as rush hour and New Year's Eve.

People are much less forgiving of hardware stores that raise prices on plywood, sandbags, water, and batteries when a hurricane is approaching. Why? Because such pricing violates the moral sense of *harm*. It feels wrong to price gouge when lives are at stake. People also don't think it is ethical for companies to charge different prices to people from different racial and ethnic groups. For example, people are often outraged when mortgage or insurance companies engage in "redlining," which results in racial minorities being charged higher rates based on where they live. Or when The Princeton Review charged more for test preparation services in low-income Asian neighborhoods compared to higher-income white neighborhoods.[26]

Why do people get enraged by such pricing strategies even though the companies are behaving like firms in standard economics textbooks, setting prices to maximize their profits? It's because it violates people's sense of *fairness*, their belief that people shouldn't be treated differently based on the color of their skin.

It's important to realize that even pricing practices that seem benign to most businesspeople strike others as outrageous. A survey by David Broockman, Gregory Ferenstein, and Neil Malhotra showed that 97 percent of technology company founders thought it was fair for florists to raise prices on holidays, and 96 percent thought it was fair for Uber to raise prices during peak times. Regular people felt quite differently, with only 53 percent and 55 percent, respectively, saying that surge pricing was fair.[27]

The fundamental issue here is that people's moral intuitions say that some goods should be sold in markets but other goods should be allocated in some other way (e.g., first come first serve, by lottery, based on need, or via government decision-making). For example, relatively few people have a problem with college students or senior citizens getting a discount on movie tickets. But almost everyone has a problem with someone selling their kidney to the highest bidder or with hospitals auctioning off COVID-19 vaccinations. People's System 1 says it's OK for companies to put a price on some things, but not others.

Anticipating System 1 responses is an important skill for managers, who want to either avoid outrage or anticipate and manage it effectively. This can help us reduce the probability of getting stuck in problematic situations. It's impossible to perfectly predict how moral intuitions will play out in an organization or the general public, but we have learned a lot from the science of the human mind. People's gut reactions may be immediate and visceral, but they are not unpredictable. Assessing whether our decisions will activate the five moral senses will help us anticipate and manage disagreement.

STRATEGIES FOR COMMUNICATING WITH OTHERS

Leadership is not just about making decisions. It is also about communicating with others. This could involve persuasion, back-and-forth conversation, or mediating a contentious discussion. For this, we have five pointers based on the ideas in this chapter. The first two are about listening and understanding, which are crucial (and undervalued) steps for effective communication. The third is about self-awareness, and the final two are about the framing of messages.

First, you need to be aware that critics outside of your company are often driven by strong moral intuitions. In Stanford's Executive Education programs, when we teach senior leaders about strategic interactions with activist critics, there are always some participants who think activists are in it for the money or are a front group for some competing business interest. Occasionally this is true. But most of the time it is a serious misimpression, and one that can lead a company to adopt ineffective or disastrous approaches for dealing with activists. However much an executive disagrees with activist critics, a much better approach is to assume that they are sincere, and to try to understand the moral foundations that underlie their position. This makes it easier to understand and respond to their moral outrage.

Second, you need to be aware that employees within your company have strong moral intuitions, which may not line up with the company's strategy or the intuitions of senior management. For example, in the late 2010s, Silicon Valley companies experienced a wave of internal protests over issues ranging from sexual harassment at Google to Facebook's decision to allow political advertisements that contain blatant lies. The protestors, as is typical for people at tech companies, gave extremely thoughtful and reasoned arguments for why the companies' policies were problematic, but underlying these arguments was an intensity of feeling that came from deep moral intuitions.

Third, you need to be aware that, like everyone else, you too are often driven by System 1 gut reactions. It does no good to be under the illusion that you're the only logical person in the room and everyone who disagrees with you is irrational or just doesn't get it.

Fourth, when trying to communicate your views to people who are driven by moral intuitions, you need to respect their intuitions. You're unlikely to sway them with a bunch of facts and data. In a series of experiments, political scientists David Broockman and Joshua Kalla attempted to reduce transphobia through a technique called "deep canvassing." In their method, the first step toward having a productive conversation is to listen nonjudgmentally, rather than immediately listing facts or calling people out.[28]

Finally, when you try to convince people who disagree with you, it is useful to frame your argument in terms of *their* moral intuitions, not *yours*. Stating your position in a way that resonates with your own intuitions might make you feel that you're right and that you've won the argument. But if you actually want to get people to agree with you, you need to frame things in a way that resonates with their intuitions. Social psychologists Matthew Feinberg and Robb Willer have shown that liberals are able to better persuade conservatives to address climate change not by focusing on the harms it causes but rather on how it makes the natural world impure.[29] Similarly, liberals wanting to convince people to accept gay marriage should present gay couples as proud and patriotic Americans who contribute to the US economy and society. This is much more effective than focusing on liberal moral foundations such as equality and fairness. Although there is no existing study to show this, we believe that gay marriage would also be more palatable to conservatives if it was framed as a way of strengthening communities via nuclear families and committed relationships.

This same general point applies for leading people within your organization. As much as you want to lead with your values, you also need to do so in a way that they find emotionally compelling.

TAKEAWAYS

1. People's ethical choices are frequently based on System 1 gut intuitions, which are quick and often emotional. System 2 reasoning that comes afterward may simply serve to rationalize the initial gut reaction.
2. There are five main moral senses: harm, fairness, ingroup, authority, and purity. Recent research has suggested a sixth moral sense: liberty.

3. Understanding System 1 responses and moral intuitions can help us:
   • anticipate and avoid moral outrage,
   • manage disagreement within our organization by clarifying which moral intuitions people are bringing to the table, and
   • persuade others by framing our arguments in terms of the moral senses they care about.
4. Why do people disagree on ethical issues in business? It is not because some people are moral and others are evil. Rather, people have different moral senses that are activated. These can be based both on personality differences as well as culture and upbringing.

SUGGESTIONS FOR FURTHER READING

If you are interested in learning more about heuristics and decision-making – not just in the context of values-based leadership – we highly recommend Daniel Kahneman's *Thinking, Fast and Slow*. For an in-depth discussion of moral intuitions and the evolutionary and cultural bases of morality, we recommend several books: *The Righteous Mind: Why Good People are Divided by Politics and Religion* by Jonathan Haidt, *Moral Tribes: Emotion, Reason, and the Gap Between Us and Them* by Joshua Greene, and *Just Babies: The Origins of Good and Evil* by Paul Bloom.

REFLECTIVE EXERCISES

1. Think about a heuristic (or rule of thumb) that's used to make decisions in your organization. Do you think this heuristic generally does well, or are there edge cases where it leads your organization to make bad decisions? Can you think of procedures that would improve decision-making?
2. Consider Haidt's six moral foundations: harm, fairness, ingroup/community, authority, purity, and liberty. Which of these moral senses are most important for your personal sense of right and wrong?
3. Think back to disagreements you've had with others in business, politics, or some other domain. Did any of these disagreements stem from differing moral intuitions? If so, is there a way you might be able to persuade others by tapping *their* moral intuitions rather than your own?

3

Self-Deception and Rationalization

In 2000, the early employees of Google were deciding on the fledgling company's core values. Software developer Paul Buchheit, who later went on to create Gmail, offered three simple words: "Don't be evil." Although this suggestion was initially dismissed, founders Sergey Brin and Larry Page ultimately embraced the phrase and included it in Google's prospectus when the company went public in 2004.

On the one hand, the slogan has a reassuring simplicity. Who would want to be evil? On the other hand, its vagueness makes it fundamentally unhelpful. When asked what "evil" means in a complex world, CEO Eric Schmidt cheekily replied: "Evil is what Sergey says is evil."[1] Of course, this could lead one to ask how Sergey determines what is evil.

But the vagueness of "Don't be evil" isn't its key limitation as a core value. An even bigger problem is that humans are wired to avoid thinking of themselves – and what they do – as evil. People engage in self-deception and rationalization, convincing themselves that they are taking the right path and doing no wrong. Ethical lapses in organizations are often products of the ways we perceive ourselves as moral beings, compare ourselves to others, and rationalize our failures to live up to our values. Consequently, leaders cannot simply tell themselves and their followers to not be evil. They need a strategy. That is what this chapter is about.

The "don't be evil" phrase didn't survive corporate restructuring when Google was reorganized as Alphabet in 2015. However, this wasn't because the phrase was overly vague. The new core value was similarly fuzzy, but more positive and affirming: "Do the right thing."[2]

GREY AREAS AND GUILT

We're going to start with two premises: (1) life is filled with moral grey areas, and (2) human beings hate feeling guilty.

Some things in life are clear-cut matters of right and wrong. For example, when the "Varsity Blues" college admissions scandal broke in 2019, almost nobody thought it was acceptable for wealthy parents to pay hundreds of thousands of dollars to the scheme's ringleader, William Singer, who faked SAT tests for their children, constructed bogus profiles of them as athletes, and bribed coaches in hopes of getting them admitted to elite universities like Georgetown, USC, Stanford, and Yale.[3]

But what about all the other ways people play the college (and business school) admissions game? Is it unethical to donate money to a university just to get an advantage? How about hiring a former admissions officer to provide advice on writing a compelling essay? What if that person heavily edits the essay? Or writes the whole thing? Is it OK to strategically do community service to pad your resume? What if you have no real interest in the service, and stop doing it as soon as you are admitted to the school of your dreams?

Different people have different answers to these questions. But for each of us, there are some things that we'd say are clearly acceptable, some that are clearly unacceptable, and some that are in the grey area in between.

Similarly, leaders of organizations make decisions in a wide variety of ethical grey areas. CFOs decide how aggressively to handle revenue recognition when accounting rules are ambiguous. Presidents of universities and other nonprofits decide how much to cater to superrich donors whose goals may be out of sync with their core mission. Anyone who negotiates makes choices about how much deception to use. People responsible for hiring may face a decision about whether to give a leg up to candidates based on connections from school, friendship, or family. And entrepreneurs, when seeking the support of investors who expect incredibly high returns, must decide how much to emphasize best-case growth projections that have little chance of being realized. Ethical grey areas are everywhere in business, and in life.

At the same time, people hate feeling guilty. Sometimes, we cannot escape guilt, because our actions are so heinous. In Dostoyevsky's classic novel *Crime and Punishment*, the main character Raskolnikov's guilt over murdering two innocent people drives him to madness and his eventual confession. But we rarely find ourselves in this position. More often, we engage in morally questionable behavior in the grey areas. In a world full of shades of grey, details matter, and our perceptions of those details play a major role in determining how we feel about ourselves and our actions. It would be great if our perceptions were always clear-eyed and reliable. Unfortunately, they aren't, because we systematically skew our interpretation of the evidence in ways that are favorable to ourselves and our ingroup.

In our attempts to reduce discomfort, we humans attempt to rationalize and justify morally questionable actions. We want to be good people and want to think of ourselves that way. This relates to one of the key insights in Chapter 1. Ethical failures in organizations are not just caused by bad people doing evil. (Google's slogan is therefore not a silver bullet.) Rather, these failures are often due to normal, reasonably good people taking the wrong path.

We will now explore why people are led astray and what we can do about it as leaders. To do so, we first need to discuss the psychological concept of *cognitive dissonance*.

REDUCING COGNITIVE DISSONANCE: HOW HUMANS RESOLVE GUILT

Cognitive dissonance is an idea introduced by the psychologist Leon Festinger in 1957.[4] Festinger argued that human beings seek internal consistency in their minds. They hate to have discordant or contradictory beliefs or ideas in their head. It is similar to how some collections of musical notes produce melodious chords whereas others are grating. People also become troubled when they do or experience something that conflicts with one of their internal beliefs. In response, they adopt various conscious and subconscious strategies to resolve and eliminate cognitive dissonance.

Of course, people had intuitions about this basic idea well before Festinger. Take, for example, Aesop's famous fable "The Fox and the Grapes," which describes the tribulations of a fox who cannot reach a bunch of sweet grapes. The fox has two discordant ideas in its head: (1) I want to eat those sweet grapes, but (2) I can't reach them. Given the physical impossibility of resolving the latter problem, the fox convinces itself that the grapes are actually sour and that it wouldn't want them anyway.

You can probably imagine various scenarios in your own life where you've experienced the phenomenon of sour grapes. Maybe you missed out on getting tickets to a big sporting event and told yourself: "It's better to watch it from my couch anyway." The flipside to "sour grapes" are "sweet lemons." Perhaps the candidate of your political party was involved in a scandal. Instead of voting for the other party, you might downplay the importance of the scandal or blame the biased news media.

Cognitive dissonance also plays an important role in how we lead with our values. Most people think to themselves: "I'm a generally good person." However, sometimes their actions contradict this statement. They may do something morally questionable for no good reason, thereby creating dissonance. People have a few options at this point. They could admit fault and own up to their mistakes. However, people often instead mitigate feelings of guilt by engaging in self-deception and rationalization.

A common way we reduce cognitive dissonance is to *deny responsibility* for unethical actions we have taken. For instance, we can claim we were simply following orders or were a "cog" in the machine, deflecting moral responsibility to superiors or a faceless bureaucracy. We can rationalize our decisions by claiming that if we did not take an unethical action then somebody else would have done it anyway. We also sometimes blame the victims of our actions, convince ourselves that they earned their fate, and understate how much they are harmed.

The end result is that, at the end of the day, we're able to look at ourselves in the mirror and think that we're pretty good people. In fact, most of us tend to think we're better than others.

ETHICAL DEFENSIVENESS

Every time we teach our class, we give our students a simple survey, asking them "Among the people in this class, what percentile do you think you fall in (0 is lowest, 50 is average, and 100 is highest) in terms of ... ." We then list a variety of positive attributes: athletic ability, quantitative skills, independence of mind, public speaking skills, ethical standards, interviewing skills, raw intelligence, and will power.

The average percentile ranking for people in a group, compared to others in that same group, must be fifty. There's no way for people to, on average, be above average. Yet we find that our students systematically rate themselves as above average on all of these traits. Their degree of self-serving bias is smallest for athletic ability, public speaking skills, raw intelligence, and quantitative skills. At the high end of the spectrum are independence of mind, will power, and the attribute we're most interested in when we give the survey: ethical standards. The average self-assessment that our students give themselves for ethical standards is typically around the 70th percentile.

Over the years, we have used this survey dozens of times for a wide variety of different audiences: Stanford MBAs, fellows in our MSx program for mid-career executives, entrepreneurs in Kenya and Ghana, prosecutors, corporate finance executives, female business leaders, libertarians in Utah, small business owners in the Bay Area, and senior executives from many different global companies. Without fail, each group exhibits the same basic pattern.[5]

One group that we haven't given the survey to is the faculty of the Stanford Graduate School of Business. We expect that the usual pattern would hold, with one possible exception: Given that business school professors care so much about their raw intelligence and quantitative skills, we conjecture that the average self-ratings on those two attributes would be especially high. Maybe even above 100.

It turns out that even people who are incarcerated believe they're relatively good. A team of psychologists and criminologists – Constantine Sedikides, Rosie Meek, Mark Alicke, and Sarah Taylor – found that English prisoners rated themselves as relatively more kind, honest, trustworthy, dependable, generous, compassionate, self-controlled, and moral, not only relative to other prisoners, but also compared to the average member of the community. When asked about how law-abiding they were, the prisoners didn't claim to be above average relative to the community – they merely rated themselves about average.[6]

Ethical defensiveness extends beyond protecting the self to protecting one's group or team. We sometimes run an experiment with our MBA students that takes advantage of the rivalry between the Stanford Graduate School of Business and Harvard Business School. We split our students into two groups and have one half read an article written by *The Stanford Daily* (Stanford's campus newspaper) about a cheating scandal at Harvard Business School and the other half read an article written by *The Harvard Crimson* (Harvard's campus newspaper) about a cheating scandal at the Stanford Graduate School of Business. However, the articles, which were written by our colleague Benoît Monin, aren't about real scandals and the text of the fake newspaper articles is *exactly* the same, except that the names Harvard and Stanford are swapped. The goal is to see whether students are motivated to protect their in-group – and derogate their out-group – when their morality is challenged.

Perhaps unsurprisingly, we find that students are more likely to call the cheating claims biased and unfair when Stanford is being accused.

Further, they engage in *confirmation bias*, the phenomenon where people pay more attention to information that confirms their prior beliefs. Our MBAs dismiss ambiguous data in the article that accuses Stanford of cheating, but find the same data fairly compelling when Harvard is being accused.

More subtly, ethical defensiveness emerges in complex and interesting ways that even self-aware individuals have a hard time recognizing. For example, after reading the article, we ask students: "If we conducted this survey at Yale, Chicago, and Berkeley, what percentage of MBAs do you think would report cheating at least once in their studies?" When they read an article accusing Stanford of cheating, most students say that *more* than half of students at Yale/Chicago/Berkeley would cheat. However, when they read an article accusing Harvard of cheating, they say that *less* than half of students at Yale/Chicago/Berkeley would cheat. This is an example of the phenomenon of *making advantageous comparisons*. Note that these three other schools are not mentioned in the article. Yet, when reading an article in which Stanford is accused, Stanford students want to think that cheating is common. On the other hand, when Harvard is accused, Stanford students want to think that cheating is rare and that Harvard Business School students are more unethical than the norm.

MORAL CREDENTIALING: WHEN DOING GOOD GIVES US LICENSE TO DO BAD

People not only want to avoid being seen as evil, but also want to be perceived as good. Accordingly, they often seek out and cling to affirmation about their own virtue. In 2001, psychologists Benoît Monin and Dale Miller developed the idea of *moral credentialing*.[7] Their argument is that when people do something good, they give themselves a pat on the back (a moral credential), and this can often give them license to do something bad in the future. In one of their experiments, they showed that giving someone an opportunity to hire a woman or a member of an underrepresented minority group for a specific job led them to make generally prejudicial comments about women and minorities later on. In a follow-up study, Monin and his coauthors found that giving Democrats the opportunity to express support for Barack Obama during the 2008 presidential campaign led them to make more racially prejudicial statements at a later point in time.[8]

Moral credentialing not only emerges in the psychology laboratory but has also been shown in large-scale field experiments on real employees.

Economists John List and Fatemeh Momeni conducted an experiment using workers on Amazon's Mechanical Turk platform, where people seek gigs for temporary work. They exposed some workers to information about a company's corporate social responsibility (CSR) efforts, thereby offering workers a moral credential. They found that the CSR information made it more likely for workers to cheat, shirk on their duties, and submit lower-quality work.[9]

Moral credentialing is a particularly acute problem in mission-driven organizations such as nonprofits, nongovernmental organizations, militaries, governments, and religious and educational institutions. When the mission of an organization is to do good for the world and not simply make profits, managers and employees may be more lax when it comes to ethical transgressions. Towards the end of this chapter, we will provide some examples where moral credentialing may have contributed to organizational failures.

ESCALATION OF COMMITMENT: FROM MINOR MISDEEDS TO MAJOR ONES

One final psychological phenomenon that we want to focus on has to do with the dynamics of wrongdoing. Most cases of major misconduct aren't one-time indiscretions. Rather, things start small and grow over time.

An example of this is the accounting fraud scandal at HealthSouth, a post-acute rehabilitation care company. Founded in 1984, HealthSouth expanded rapidly and eventually reached the Fortune 500. In the 1990s, the company's leaders – including CEO Richard Scrushy, CFO Aaron Beam, and other finance executives – realized they were about to fall short of Wall Street's expectations, so they started to manipulate their earnings.

They started with relatively small changes to their accounting practices. Some of these changes were legal and they even disclosed some to their auditors. For instance, Scrushy and Beam overstated the amount of revenue they would collect from accounts receivable. But over time, the scale of the fraud grew. They lied to their auditors and put thousands of completely fake entries on the books. By the time the scheme was discovered in 2003, the magnitude of the fraud was over $4 billion. Several of the executives went to jail and Richard Scrushy lost a $2.8 billion civil suit.[10]

HealthSouth illustrates an important phenomenon: *escalation of commitment*. People who make a bad decision often don't pull back from that decision, but rather continue on the same path, even ramping up over

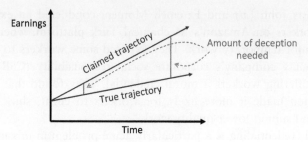

FIGURE 3.1. **Escalation of earnings manipulation**

time. This phenomenon isn't just about ethical misdeeds. It also can include, for example, pouring more and more money into a failing investment, rather than treating losses as a sunk cost and jumping ship.

Psychologists have offered many explanations for escalation of commitment. Given that our focus is on unethical decisions, three of these explanations are particularly important.

First, it's easier to take multiple small steps towards wrongdoing, ramping up gradually, because each incremental step isn't much worse than what we've already done.

Second, once we've done something unethical, to stop doing it means admitting that we are in the wrong. It's hard to admit this to ourselves. It's even harder to admit it to investors, regulators, and legal authorities. Often, people find it easier to continue and even increase their misbehavior.

Third, unethical behavior often creates the need for additional unethical behavior. As shown in Figure 3.1, a company that tries to overstate its growth rate initially only needs to do a bit of earnings manipulation. But over time the gap between the fabricated earnings and the true earnings grows, and much more fraud is needed to make up the difference.

Moreover, engaging in fraud often requires a cover-up and an ever-growing web of deceit in order to fool investors, auditors, and government regulators. It also often requires lying to coworkers who aren't in on the scam, as well as friends and family.

To illustrate the concepts in this chapter, we'll now discuss some recent scandals in businesses and organizations.

CASE STUDIES OF ORGANIZATIONAL FAILURES

It seems as if every few months we read about a major ethical crisis within an organization. As we've argued throughout this chapter, it would be simplistic to think that these failures were simply due to evil people hatching nefarious plots. Rather, many organizational failures are caused by fundamentally good people trying to rationalize bad behavior. At the core of many of these crises are failures of leadership.

The UNC Cheating Scandal

In the early 2010s a scandal broke which revealed that officials at the University of North Carolina-Chapel Hill (UNC) had created an elaborate scheme in which student athletes received credit for bogus classes so they could maintain their eligibility to compete. These classes often required essentially no effort. For instance, one class had no lectures, did not require attendance, had no instructor, and required students to complete a one-page paper to receive course credit. From 1993 to 2011 the scheme involved more than 3,100 UNC students, over half of whom were athletes, including many from the football and basketball teams.

Dr. Jeanette Boxill, an academic counselor for UNC's women's basketball wrote in an email to Deborah Crowder, an administrator who ran the fake classes: "Hi Debby, Yes, a D will be fine; that's all she needs. I didn't look at the paper but figured it was a recycled one as well, but I couldn't figure from where! Thanks for whatever you can do." Given the research on moral credentialing that we mentioned earlier in the chapter, it is interesting to note that Boxill is a moral philosopher who directed the Parr Center for Ethics at UNC.[11]

On the surface, the scandal may seem like a classic case of universities bending and breaking the rules in college sports, seeking athletic glory and huge amounts of revenue, and not really caring about whether "student-athletes" get an education along the way.

However, investigations revealed that some of the people at the center of the UNC scandal had much more complex motivations and ethical rationalizations. Crowder, for example, was widely respected as being someone who cared deeply about students. She especially felt sympathy for those who were struggling academically at UNC and believed that she was doing the right thing by engaging in the scheme. In a 2004 email, she described her approach as follows: "[many different] students come in for advising, or cause us problems, or are wonderful, or whatever, but sometimes I think the athletes get too much scrutiny in relation to the average student population. That being said, we try to accommodate [athletes'] schedules, just as we do the single moms, or the students who have to work two jobs to stay in school."[12]

Theranos

In the early 2010s, Theranos appeared to be well on its way to becoming the next great Silicon Valley success story. Founded in 2003, the company's goal was to develop a revolutionary, highly portable blood-testing machine that only required a few drops of blood. Its founder and CEO, Elizabeth Holmes, followed the path of many tech visionaries. She studied chemical engineering at Stanford, but dropped out at the age of 19 to follow her passion and build her company. The prospects seemed bright, and Holmes used her Stanford connections to recruit an all-star board of directors, including retired generals, former senators and cabinet secretaries, and CEOs of major companies.

By 2015, Theranos was worth over $9 billion, and many people were excited about the prospect that its technology would dramatically improve accessibility of crucial medical tests, thereby saving countless lives, while making a ton of money along the way.

Later that same year, everything came crashing down. John Carreyrou of *The Wall Street Journal* published an incredibly well-reported article showing that the vast majority of Theranos's tests weren't run on the company's own machines, but rather on equipment that was purchased from the German company Siemens. Later, more details came out. Theranos's machines were unreliable and the company had deceived regulators about its tests. The company had created a fake laboratory to show off to investors and government officials, including Vice President Joe Biden, who visited in 2015 and came away impressed, describing it as "the laboratory of the future." As we write this, Elizabeth Holmes and the company's President and COO Sunny Balwani are set to go on trial for wire fraud and conspiracy to defraud doctors, patients, and investors. Theranos shut down and its investors lost all their money.[13]

How did this happen? We probably will never know exactly what was going on inside the minds of Theranos's executives. So we can't rule out the possibility that they intended all along to build a fraudulent enterprise. But we think a more likely explanation is that for many years they truly believed they would succeed in revolutionizing blood testing. Over time, while outsiders' expectations for the company ramped up, insiders gradually learned that their technology wasn't on a path to working. Theranos's leaders took the Silicon Valley culture of "fake it till you make it" to an extreme, engaging in ever-greater amounts of deception, and hoping that ultimately they would prevail. They may well have told themselves that this deception was justified because their company's mission was about improving people's health, in contrast to other tech startups that were just trying to create the next food delivery app.

The fall of Theranos also speaks to the issue of moral credentialing. As described by Carreyrou, Holmes constantly spoke about Theranos's social mission of improving and streamlining testing. This resulted in her and her employees justifying unethical actions in the service of the broader goal of disrupting and improving the health care industry.

STRATEGIES TO COMBAT SELF-DECEPTION: THE PERSONAL LEVEL

So far, this chapter has been fairly negative. We've discussed the ways in which people and organizations take unethical actions yet manage to preserve a positive image of themselves. However, it is not enough to point out problems. It's also important to explain how to solve and address psychological biases.

HealthSouth, UNC, and Theranos are extreme cases. But the fact that they exemplify biases and rationalizations that psychologists have documented in the behavior of regular people should give all of us pause. A key takeaway is that we should be skeptical of our decisions and our motivations. Unfortunately, it's difficult to maintain that skepticism in our day-to-day lives, and it's even harder to have it serve as an effective check on our behavior. We humans are simply too skillful at painting ourselves in a positive light. Thus, it's necessary to have specific tools that help us live according to our values. Here we'll discuss three such tools.

Bright-Line Rules

Clayton Christensen, who developed the theory of disruptive innovation in his classic book *The Innovator's Dilemma*, made an interesting observation about living an ethical life: "It's easier to hold to your principles 100 percent of the time than it is to hold to them 98 percent of the time."[14]

There's a lot of truth to this. If you always stick to a rule, it's pretty difficult to concoct a rationalization for why it's OK to violate it "just this once." And escalation into major wrongdoing can't occur if you never take the first step on the path away from your principles.

But Christensen's approach only works if it's possible to translate your core values into clear rules that eliminate any possible grey areas. Christensen illustrated his 98 percent vs. 100 percent idea with an example drawn from his experiences as a basketball player and as a member of the Church of Jesus Christ of Latter-day Saints. He was an excellent athlete, but early in his life he decided that one of his personal commitments as a Mormon was that he wouldn't play sports on Sundays. When he was a student at Oxford, his basketball team made it to the national championship game, which was on a Sunday. Christensen would have loved to play and didn't want to let his teammates down, but he decided to stick with his bright-line rule of not playing on Sundays. This surely was a difficult sacrifice to make, but his decision was made easier by the fact that the rule "don't play sports on Sundays" is very simple and clear. There's no grey area there.

For decisions where your core values give unambiguous guidance, bright-line rules are quite useful. They are particularly helpful when you can predict things well in advance, such as the day that a basketball game will take place. It may even make sense to intentionally create bright lines for situations where your values might not yield a clear-cut answer.

But although bright lines are useful, they're not enough. Even if you commit to a bunch of bright lines, you're still going to encounter plenty of situations where none of them apply. Grey areas are inevitable. There also will be times where your bright-line rules come into conflict with each other. And, if you're like most people, you'll sometimes fail to live up to your values and cross the lines that you established for yourself.

The good news is that doing the wrong thing once doesn't mean we're doomed to do it forever. For example, many people submit a couple of improper expense reports without ramping up to major embezzlement. Escalation of commitment isn't inevitable.

What we need is a plan for how to deal with the difficult and messy situations that arise when we, as fallible human beings, grapple with a world full of grey areas.

The New York Times Test

One rule of thumb that many people suggest is to avoid doing anything you wouldn't want to have exposed on the front page of a major newspaper. This rule is sometimes called the newspaper test or the *New York Times* test.

This test has three nice features. First, it reminds us that not all secrets stay secret. Second, it encourages us to take the perspective of others, who aren't likely to buy into whatever rationalizations we might use to justify our behavior. Third, it taps into our emotions, specifically our fear of being publicly shamed.

But the test also has serious drawbacks. Most misbehavior does not make the front page of any newspaper, so the test feels hypothetical rather than immediately relevant. It's also easy to distort. For example, many business people are skeptical of reporters and think they're just out to make companies look bad. For people who feel this way it's easy to discount any possible criticism by the news media by saying it's superficial, judgmental, and biased towards negativity.

Ultimately, we think the newspaper test is more about reputation management than adherence to one's core values.

The Friends and Family Test

A more compelling approach is to ask: "How will my close friends and family react if I tell them what I'm doing?" This has several advantages. Presumably your friends and family share many of your core values. And surely they'd be willing to listen and try to understand the nuances of your decisions, rather than rushing to superficial judgment. Perhaps most importantly, the test is emotionally compelling and far from hypothetical, because engaging in seriously unethical behavior often involves hiding it from friends and family.

That said, the test does have its own drawbacks and weaknesses. Sometimes our friends and family are our accomplices and enablers. It's also possible to deceive ourselves about how our friends and family might respond, telling ourselves that they'd be fine with our behavior, when in fact they wouldn't. Of course, if you think they'd approve of what you're doing, then you might as well go ahead and tell them about it. And if you hesitate to tell them ... well, maybe that's a warning sign, because you suspect that they actually wouldn't approve.

STRATEGIES TO COMBAT SELF-DECEPTION: THE ORGANIZATIONAL LEVEL

Homer's *Odyssey* is an epic Greek poem about the struggle of the hero Odysseus to return home to his family after the Trojan War. His trek is a metaphor for the journeys we take as leaders. To achieve his goal, Odysseus must confront numerous obstacles, including six-headed monsters, cannibals, and a giant Cyclops. In one of the most well-known scenes, Odysseus must sail with his men past treacherous rocks guarded by the Sirens, mythical creatures with the heads of women and the bodies of birds. They sing magical and beautiful songs that tempt sailors to steer toward the rocks and sink their ships.

The Sirens represent the temptations of greed and power we all face in our leadership journeys. We know we should resist them, but sometimes their songs are too powerful. We are sometimes drawn to cheat, steal, and harm others. Yet, Odysseus devises a brilliant plan to navigate his team to safety. He puts wax in his men's ears so they cannot hear the Sirens' songs and become distracted. However, Odysseus wants to hear the music, so he asks his men to tie him to the mast so he does not jump overboard. As they sail past the Sirens, Odysseus screams, begging his men to untie him, but they cannot hear his pleas and the ship passes through unscathed.

Notice how Odysseus is able to overcome the Sirens' temptation. He doesn't simply will himself and his men to resist. Rather, he develops thoughtful strategies *before* facing temptation, knowing that willpower alone will not be sufficient. Similarly, leaders cannot simply tell themselves and their followers to do the right thing. The command "don't be evil" is not enough. Likewise, it doesn't do much good to try to change human psychology, for example by trying to train people not to have self-serving biases. Even people who have learned about biases and rationalizations are still prone to them. Instead, leaders must implement *institutions* – rules, policies, and organizational structures – that guide people to take ethical actions. These institutions are the balls of wax in the ears, the tough rope that keeps people tied to the mast.

We'll now give some examples of institutions that can address common ethical biases. Of course, your organization will face unique challenges that require the construction of tailor-made institutions. Our goal here is not to tell you the perfect solution – that would be impossible, without knowing the details of your organization. Nor will we give a lengthy laundry list of potential solutions, only some of which will be useful. Rather our goal is to provide general intuitions for thinking about institutional design, so that you can make wise decisions about what will work best for the organizations you lead.

Broadly speaking, there are four types of levers that can be used to help people avoid taking actions that are out of step with their values and the organization's values: reducing opportunities to benefit from misconduct, increasing penalties, increasing the chances of being caught, and providing off-ramps for people who start on the wrong path so they can exit rather than escalating their misbehavior.

One general approach to institutional design is to limit conflicts of interest and thereby reduce opportunities to benefit from misconduct.

When people are conflicted, they often rationalize unethical choices, because they are incentivized to do so. For instance, one factor that contributed to the HealthSouth accounting scandal was that the CEO appointed a compliant board of directors. The company did business with board members, and the board was compensated with stock options. Consequently, the board had little incentive to provide oversight and audit the firm's questionable accounting practices.

In the "Varsity Blues" scandal, a key contributing factor was that individual coaches at many universities had tremendous influence over admissions decisions for recruited athletes. The ringleader, William Singer, found that he could create a conflict of interest for the coaches, by offering bribes or donations for those who got his clients' kids admitted. In the wake of the scandal, some universities moved to eliminate this sort of conflict of interest by taking donor relations and admissions decisions out of coaches' hands.

A second general approach to institutional design is to monitor employees and executives whose financial compensation is determined by high-powered incentives, such as sales commissions and stock options. Such incentives are a key tool for motivating performance in many firms. However, they also can tempt people into lying and cheating in order to achieve metrics and objectives. Well-designed commission structures balance these tradeoffs by introducing penalties for unethical actions. For instance, one problem with sales-based commissions is that employees may have incentives to deceive customers. Randomized audits can reduce this temptation. With respect to both commissions and stock options, companies can institute clawback provisions that allow gains to be confiscated if people are found to be engaging in unethical behavior.

Within a monitoring system, it often makes sense to give people incentives to come clean and stop any unethical behavior they are engaging in. This can be done by having smaller punishments for those who turn themselves in than for those who are caught in the act. Of course, there is a tradeoff, because smaller punishments are less effective for ex ante deterrence of misbehavior. Moreover, reduced punishments go against people's moral intuition that bad things are done by bad people, who should be punished. From our perspective, though, a lot of corporate wrongdoing is done by decent people who start off small and who are initially able to rationalize and mislead themselves about their actions. Over time these self-deceptions may be harder to maintain, and it is important to design an off-ramp they can take rather than escalating to greater misdeeds.

One final thing to note is that the organizational and institutional levers that we discussed here have to do with the structure of incentives and formal procedures for individual-level decisions. For leaders who wish to promote ethical behavior, an equally important aspect of organizational design is corporate culture and norms for group-level decision making. That is the topic that we will turn to in the next chapter.

TAKEAWAYS

1. People dislike feeling cognitive dissonance, especially when our unethical actions conflict with our image of ourselves as ethical people. To reduce discomfort, we instinctively rationalize and justify unethical actions.
2. Rationalization can take various forms, including denial of responsibility for our actions and minimizing the harms to others.
3. People systematically believe they are better than others. And when we feel that we have good moral credentials, we feel free to take unethical actions.
4. Small transgressions don't always stay small, but sometimes can escalate into major misdeeds.
5. The remedy for self-deception and rationalization is not simply to increase willpower or preach doctrines such as "don't be evil."
    *   For individuals, a useful test is to ask how one's friends and family would react to our actions.
    *   For leaders of organizations, it is important to design rules and institutions that shape people's incentives and constrain their behavior to discourage them from taking unethical actions.

SUGGESTIONS FOR FURTHER READING

Max Bazerman and Ann Tenbrunsel's *Blind Spots: Why We Fail to Do What's Right and What to Do About It* is a deep dive into individual-level psychological biases that can lead to unethical decisions. For a shorter review of similar concepts, you can read Max Bazerman, George Loewenstein, and Don Moore's *Harvard Business Review* article "Why Good Accountants Do Bad Audits." John Carreyrou's chronicling of the Theranos scandal in *Bad Blood: Secrets and Lies in a Silicon Valley Startup* touches on many themes of this chapter. As you read the book, see how many of the psychological phenomena you can spot throughout the narrative. You can also perform a similar exercise while watching the

Academy Award winning film *Spotlight* about the Catholic Church's sexual abuse scandal.

REFLECTIVE EXERCISES

1. Think of an ethical lapse in the business world that you have personally witnessed or read about in the news. Can any of the psychological phenomena in this chapter help you better understand why people failed to do the right thing?
2. Can you think of institutional or organizational solutions that could have prevented the ethically problematic situation? In particular, what incentives or company policies could have counteracted the psychological biases at play?

4

The Power of the Situation

About twenty miles from Stanford University, across the marshlands of the San Francisco Bay, is the Tesla Factory in Fremont, California. This five million square foot building produces some of the most cutting-edge and technologically advanced vehicles in the world, including Tesla's four mass-market "sexy" cars: Models S, 3, X, and Y.

This factory was not always known for making such high-quality products. In the early 1980s, the plant was owned by General Motors (GM) and it assembled models such as the Buick Regal and the GMC Caballero. GM closed the plant in 1982 due to numerous labor and quality control issues. Workers sometimes showed up drunk, or failed to show up at all. They sabotaged cars by, for example, placing bottles inside the doors that would rattle around. Sometimes this was so they could make repairs and earn overtime pay. Other times it was just to annoy the customers who bought the cars. Years later, in an interview on *This American Life*, the United Auto Workers (UAW) union leader for the plant remarked, "It was considered the worst workforce in the automobile industry in the United States. And it was a reputation that was well earned."

At the same time, Toyota was looking to expand into the US market and gain a foothold in US manufacturing. Toyota made GM an offer. They could reopen the plant as a joint venture and the assembly line would make both Toyota and GM vehicles. This would help Toyota establish a US manufacturing base shielded from import restrictions, while GM could learn about Toyota's renowned lean manufacturing practices. In 1984, the plant was reopened as the joint venture NUMMI, which stood for New United Motor Manufacturing, Inc.

The managers of NUMMI made an interesting decision. They rehired 85 percent of the GM workforce. They sent some, including supervisors, to Japan to learn the "Toyota Way." Among other reforms, workers were taught the importance of teamwork. The workers were instructed to wear the same uniforms and eat together in the same cafeteria. They also were incentivized to stop the assembly line if they saw problems. The emphasis was on long-term quality and not simply short-term quantity. The first car produced at the plant, a new version of the Chevy Nova, was character-ized by extremely high build quality and efficient production.[1]

The NUMMI story is fascinating if you think about it. These were the *same* workers in the *same* physical location. But when the culture changed, so did their performance. The lesson of NUMMI is that people's choices – ethical and otherwise – are often not driven by their inherent natures. Rather, people are products of their situations and circumstances. Put in the right environment people thrive. Put in a bad system they fail to do what is right.

One thing that may strike you about the way we told the story of NUMMI is that we didn't talk about the individuals – from Toyota, GM, and the UAW – who led the organizational change. This was intentional on our part, because the key to this story is the organization, not the individuals. But this way of describing things stands in stark contrast with how people often talk about leadership, especially in Silicon Valley.

The archetypical Silicon Valley entrepreneur is a maverick, who starts with a brilliant but quirky insight and then relentlessly builds a company, persevering through tough times and ultimately succeeding in heroic triumph. The Valley's stories and legends are mainly about individual leaders, as exemplified by the title of Guy Raz's popular podcast on entrepreneurship, "How I Built This."

Of course, the idea of the heroic individual didn't originate in Silicon Valley. It has a very long cultural legacy. It's the image of rugged individu-alism and the iconic cowboy in the American West. It's the path of the lead character in many action movies, from *Star Wars* to *The Hunger Games* and from *Moana* to *Black Panther*. It's the life story of literary protagon-ists, from Prince Hal in William Shakespeare's *Henry IV* to Dagny Taggart in Ayn Rand's *Atlas Shrugged*. It's the way we talk about inspirational activists like Rosa Parks and Nelson Mandela. It's what Apple tapped into in its famous ad campaigns "1984" and "Think Different." And it's the implicit subtext of many business school cases, in which founders and CEOs look out of airplane windows and ponder key strategic decisions about the direction of their companies and their lives.

When it comes to matters of right and wrong, Western cultures – and especially US culture – tend to treat people as autonomous actors who are wholly responsible for their own individual decisions. Rodin's *The Thinker* isn't just thinking – he's doing it alone, up on his pedestal. Also alone on pedestals are statues of great leaders, whether of social movements or of countries. Visionary business leaders typically aren't put on literal pedestals, but they're surely put on metaphorical ones.

On the flip side, when we think of villains, whether in politics or business, we tend to see their behavior as a product of flaws in their individual moral character. Think of Richard Nixon, the paranoid and criminal former President of the United States; or Martin Shkreli, the greedy "pharma bro" who jacked up prices of critically needed drugs; or Bernie Madoff, who created a massive financial Ponzi scheme that tore apart his family and community; or Eike Batista, the vain and ultra-competitive Brazilian natural resources mogul who went from being the seventh richest man in the world to a prison cell as his business empire collapsed amid revelations of financial fraud and bribery.

Stories of heroism and villainy vividly convey a society's values. They can inspire us to do good, even if we don't act on quite the same grand scale as the legendary figures. But, like most myths, these stories are incomplete as descriptions of human behavior. In particular, they dramatically understate how much our actions are shaped by situational factors. Whereas the archetypical hero has the strength of character to do the right thing even in difficult circumstances, psychologists have compellingly shown that an individual's behavior is powerfully influenced by their social context.

Psychologists have also shown that people misperceive the causes of others' behavior: We overestimate the importance of their character and underestimate the influence of the situational context. This is called the *fundamental attribution error*.[2] We mistakenly categorize others as good guys and bad guys, heroes and villains, when in fact most people are like the autoworkers at the NUMMI plant, just going through life, responding to the circumstances in which they find themselves. Seeing how people are influenced by their situation doesn't just lead to a more accurate understanding of their behavior. It also has profound implications for organizational design and for our own individual choices.

In this chapter, we explore the power of the situation. In the previous two chapters, we examined how *internal* factors such as gut intuitions and rationalizations shape people's ethical choices. Now we will examine how the *external* environment affects people's decisions. Perhaps this seems obvious. Everyone knows that peer pressure, conformity, and obedience to authority figures can place stress on our ethical choices. However, we will also discuss more subtle situational pressures that are difficult to detect, and therefore hard to guard against. Specifically, we will explore how the perception – and misperception – of social norms can lead individuals and organizations down the wrong path. As in the last chapter, our goal is not only to point out human flaws and frailties, but also to offer solutions and tips for organizational leadership and personal decision-making.

TWO STUDIES: BAD NEWS AND GOOD NEWS

To motivate the lessons in this chapter, we'd like to tell you about two famous academic studies. One offers bad news about the power of situational pressures, but the other provides some good news. Personally, we always like to hear the bad news first.

In 1970, Princeton psychologists John Darley and Dan Batson conducted a study on forty seminary students.[3] These students were in training to become religious leaders, so they were committed to studying ethics and leading ethical lives. Half of the subjects were asked to prepare a speech on the vocational careers of seminary students. The other half were asked to prepare a speech about the parable of The Good Samaritan. In this parable, Jesus responds to a question about what it means to love one's neighbor by telling the story of a Samaritan who helps out a Jewish traveler who had been robbed and beaten on the side of the road. The Samaritan assists the man despite the fact that Samaritans and Jews generally did not get along at the time. Jesus's message is a core principle not only of Judeo-Christian ethics, but of nearly all religious (and many secular) traditions: It is not enough to "do no harm" – one must also actively help those who are in need.

The Princeton researchers had an accomplice. They hired an actor to sit slumped and groaning on the side of the road as the seminary students left the experimental laboratory on the way to deliver their speeches. Darley and Batson asked the question: Did the subject matter of the speech affect the seminary students' decisions to *actually* help the man in distress on the side of the road? They found a difference, but they could not statistically distinguish the effect. Fifty-three percent of the students who were preparing a speech about The Good Samaritan helped the man on the side of the road, whereas 29 percent of the students who were preparing a speech about post-seminary careers did so.

Darley and Batson also included another condition in their experimental design. They placed one-third of the subjects in a "high-hurry" group, telling them they were already late for their appointment to give the speech. In two other conditions, the experimenters ratcheted down the time pressure: a medium-hurry group and a low-hurry group. They found that this time pressure manipulation was much more powerful than the content of the speech. In the low-hurry condition, 63 percent of students helped the man on the side of the road. This figure dropped to 45 percent in the medium-hurry condition and only 10 percent in the high-hurry condition. The helping rate in the low-hurry condition was statistically significantly higher than the rates in the other two conditions combined.

What is the main lesson from this experiment? The seminary students had been studying ethical principles for a long time. They hoped to lead lives where they communicated these principles to others. You would think that nearly all of them would have helped someone in distress on the side of the road, particularly while preparing to deliver a speech about the importance of helping one's neighbors, including those who are in distress on the side of a road.

However, like most humans, these students' actions were a product of situational factors. When under time pressure, they were more likely to walk past the person in need in order to get to their next important appointment. No one would call these students bad people. Far from it – they were committed to living lives of principle and purpose. But even good people can fail to live up to their values when placed in the wrong circumstances.

The particular contextual factor that Darley and Batson identified – time pressure – is an important contributor to many unethical decisions. For example, college students are more likely to plagiarize an assignment if they are hurrying to submit it at the last minute. Similarly, many cases of corporate fraud occur when employees feel rushed to deliver results.

Now let's move on to the more optimistic study. In 1961, psychologist Stanley Milgram wanted to understand why a large number of Germans actively participated in the Holocaust, the largest mass murder in human history.[4] He posted flyers around New Haven, Connecticut seeking participants for "a scientific study of memory and learning." Upon arrival at a Yale University laboratory, a participant would be told that previous studies had examined how rewards affect learning, whereas this one was going to determine the effect of punishments. A fellow participant, who was actually an accomplice of the experimental team, would show up and the two of them would draw straws to determine who would be the "teacher" and who would be the "learner." The real subject was always put in the teacher role. The subject would read pairs of words, and then ask the learner to press a button corresponding to the correct match. A learner who made a mistake or failed to give an answer would receive an electric shock. To give the shocks, metal cuffs were placed on the learner's arms. The experimenter would take the subject to the next room over, where the subject would sit while reading words and administering shocks. In reality, the shock machine was fake and the accomplice would pretend to feel pain, but the real subject didn't know that.

To administer the electric "shocks," the subject used a box with a series of levers. Each lever corresponded to a slightly stronger shock, starting with 15 volts, then 30, 45, and so on, up to 450 volts, a level at which electricity can break down the insulating properties of human skin, allowing the current to reach muscles and organs. For each wrong answer, the experimenter told the subject to "move one level higher on the shock generator." Below the levers were labels. The first few were labeled "Slight Shock," the next few "Moderate Shock," and other categories, up to "Danger: Severe Shock" and "XXX."

As the intensity of the shocks increased, the subject would hear the learner shouting in agony, begging that the experiment be stopped, and ultimately going silent, presumably because the learner was unconscious or dead. If the subject objected to giving a shock, the experimenter would firmly insist, using a sequence of prods like "The experiment requires that you continue" and "You have no other choice, you *must* go on."

Milgram surveyed psychology majors as well as his academic colleagues and found that they overwhelmingly believed subjects would give relatively small shocks. They expected that only a few subjects, the true sociopaths, would give the maximum 450 volts. This expectation was dramatically wrong. Only a tiny minority of subjects stopped below 120 volts (the strength of household electrical current in the United States) and 65 percent of them went all the way up to the 450-volt shock. They didn't do this happily. Indeed, many were visibly upset, but they nonetheless gave the shocks. (A separate question is whether this experiment was ethical in the first place, as it used deception to place people in a highly distressing situation.)

Milgram's experiment has been the subject of countless debates and interpretations. One reaction that some people have is to think that if they had participated in the experiment they would be one of the few people who only gave a small shock. But obviously most of us can't be in that small minority, and for each of us the best guess is probably that there's about a 65 percent chance that we would have gone up to 450 volts.

Of course, as we learned in Chapter 3, we tend to think of ourselves as "above average" when it comes to matters of ethics.

Another common reaction is to conclude that humans are monstrous creatures who are capable of doing great evil. Recall that a major goal of Milgram's experiment was to understand the Holocaust. In our view, this interpretation is partially correct. Ordinary people are, indeed, capable of committing terrible wrongs.

At this point, you might be wondering: Wasn't this study supposed to be the one with good news? While many people know about the initial results from the Milgram experiment, most don't know about additional tests Milgram conducted to see what he could do to *decrease* people's willingness to administer shocks. He found various techniques that helped. For example, when the experiment was conducted in a regular office building rather than at Yale, only 48 percent of subjects exhibited full compliance and gave shocks all the way up to 450 volts. When the experimenter was physically distant, running the experiment by telephone rather than in person, full compliance fell to around 20 percent. A similar drop-off occurred if the experimenter was a regular person, who didn't have the status and authority of a scientist.

One of the most effective techniques was when Milgram hired two other actors to pretend to be experimental subjects who stood up to the experimenter and refused to administer high levels of shocks. In this condition, only 10 percent of actual subjects exhibited full compliance. So the good news is that situational pressures cut both ways. People can exhibit moral courage if they know they are not alone. All they require is some social proof that others are in their corner. We will revisit this theme later in the chapter where we discuss ways to design organizational structures so that people have social support to do the right thing.

The most important lesson of the Milgram experiment is not that people are horrible, but rather that people are profoundly influenced by the power of the situation. Although people can do wrong when placed in the wrong situation, there is also reason for hope, because situations can be designed to encourage good behavior.

WHAT'S EVERYONE ELSE DOING?

The two studies described above examined situational factors that influence ethical behavior: time pressure and authority. However, probably the biggest drivers of moral decision-making are social norms. Norms are essentially the "rules of the game" that govern social interactions between people. Norms were clearly important in the transition from the dysfunctional General Motors Fremont Assembly to the highly efficient NUMMI plant. In 1982, the norm at the GM plant was that manufacturing quality and pride in work were unimportant. Just two years later, the norms at NUMMI stressed teamwork and discipline.

Sometimes norms are *explicit*. For instance, if you're at a restaurant and you see a drawing of a cigarette on the wall with a big "X" through it, this means that the norm is to not smoke. Of course, in some situations the actual norm may diverge from the formal rules. For example, while we were writing this chapter in the summer of 2020, one of the authors (Ken) took a family road trip through the Western United States and saw that in many places people ignored signs telling them to wear masks to reduce the spread of COVID-19.

In fact, most of the time there isn't a sign or formal policy to tell us about norms: They are *implicit*, which means they are unwritten and have to be inferred from the behavior of others. For example, think of a time when you were invited to a wedding or religious ceremony from a culture that was unfamiliar to you. It was probably interesting and also a moment of pride and joy, especially if the ceremony was for one of your close friends. But maybe you also approached the event with a bit of trepidation and a bunch of questions: What sort of clothing should I wear? When should I arrive? Where should I sit? During the ceremony, when should I sit and when should I stand? Are there parts of the ceremony that it would be inappropriate for me to take part in? If there's a reception with dancing, is my style of dancing acceptable? And, more generally, how do I join in the fun and joy without accidentally doing something inappropriate, offending people, or making a fool of myself?

Fortunately, most of these questions are easy to answer. All you need to do is look around at what others are doing and imitate their behavior. If they sit, I sit. If they stand, I stand. If they kneel, I kneel. If everyone else is hanging out and chatting with each other rather than paying attention to the ceremony, it's probably fine for me to do that too. And if others are silent, with their heads bowed, that's the right course of action for me as well.

This approach doesn't just work for weddings and religious ceremonies. It works for all sorts of social situations: your first day at a new school, first middle school dance, first time walking across an intersection in Manhattan, first time buying food in a bazaar, and first day at a new job. Just look around, see what others are doing, do what they do, and it's pretty likely that everything will turn out fine. Humans are amazing social creatures and have an uncanny ability to pick up on norms as guidelines for behavior. And, at least most of the time, doing so helps us make appropriate decisions.

Problems can arise, however, if we perceive unethical decisions as being the norm. The psychologist Robert Cialdini and his research team conducted a study in the Petrified Forest National Park in Arizona that illustrated the power of norms in shaping behavior.[5] The park had a problem with visitors stealing pieces of 225-million-year-old petrified wood to take home as souvenirs. There was a sign at the park that seemed to do little good: "Your heritage is being vandalized every day by theft losses of petrified wood of fourteen tons a year, mostly a small piece at a time." The researchers' hypothesis was that the sign actually *encouraged* wood theft: Fourteen tons ... a small piece at a time ... wow, it sure sounds like lots of people think it's OK to steal a bit of petrified wood. It's more like a scavenger hunt, not shoplifting!

Cialdini and his colleagues ran an experiment altering the park's signage and found that it made a difference. When the sign read "Please don't remove the petrified wood chips," less than 2 percent of specially marked wood chips were stolen. When the sign read "Many past visitors have removed the petrified wood from the park, changing the state of the petrified forest," about 8 percent of wood chips were stolen. When theft is communicated as an accepted norm, it becomes less socially deviant.

These ideas have been applied to prosocial behaviors as well. One experiment found that people are more likely to vote in elections if you tell them that voting is a common activity rather than emphasizing how many people don't vote.[6] Similarly, hotels often display signs saying that many people choose to reuse their towels to save water. The goal of this communication strategy is to convince you that getting a fresh set of clean towels every day is a deviant, anti-environmental behavior, rather than a hygienic, commonly accepted norm.

At the same time, although people are skilled at inferring implicit norms, they are not perfect at it. Problems often arise when people *mis*perceive norms, thinking that a certain belief about ethical behavior is prevalent, when in fact it isn't. In the remainder of this chapter, we will dive into how people misperceive norms and what we can do about it as leaders.

TWO WAYS PEOPLE MISPERCEIVE NORMS

I'm Just Doing What Everyone Else Is Doing

One justification people often give for their behavior is that they are just doing what most others do. In other words, they are simply following a norm. But one thing psychologists have learned is that people misperceive norms in predictable ways. For instance, people who do something tend to think "everyone else is doing it." The technical term for this phenomenon is the *false consensus effect*, or the tendency for people who engage in a behavior to be more likely to think that others engage in that behavior than those who do not. The same is true for attitudes.[7]

The precise technical definition of false consensus effect is simply the difference between the two groups' perceptions. The key takeaway for leaders is that people often tend to see their own choices and beliefs as common and sometimes overestimate how much others agree with them. For instance, some people prefer beer and others prefer wine. Beer drinkers generally think that more people like beer, whereas wine drinkers think that more people like wine.

The false consensus effect shows up in business situations as well. Every year, we give our students a survey that describes different ethical dilemmas in the workplace. The dilemmas were designed by social psychologists Frank Flynn and Scott Wiltermuth to be situations in which reasonable people could disagree about the right thing to do.[8] For example, one of them reads as follows:

You are in charge of testing a new software package that your company has recently developed. It will be launched in a week, which means you will need to set up round-the-clock testing before then. You have to assign people to two teams: one daytime shift and one graveyard shift. You decide to let your married employees off of the graveyard shift because many of them have kids.

We then ask the students two questions. First, we ask whether they think the decision is ethical or unethical. Second, we ask what percentage of their fellow MBAs taking the survey would think the decision is ethical or unethical. For each group in the first question – those who thought it was ethical and those who thought it was unethical – we take the average of the estimates in the second question. We consistently find that those who think it was ethical believe that most of their peers agree with them that it was ethical, while at the same time, those who think it was unethical believe that most of their peers agree with them that it was unethical. This is a strong form of the false consensus effect – not only is there a difference between the perceptions of the two groups, but each group actually believes they are in the majority.

Why do people exhibit the false consensus effect? One potential reason is that people project their own beliefs onto others. They want to believe that their ideas and behaviors are normal, not deviant. Another potential reason is related to the availability heuristic, which we described in Chapter 2. We tend to hang out with people who are like us (a phenomenon sociologists call homophily), so the behaviors we engage in and the beliefs we hold seem commonplace and are available to us in our memories.

Why does this matter for leadership? One reason we (and our followers) engage in unethical behavior is that we mistakenly believe that an unethical course of action is common practice. Further, we are motivated to perceive things this way because we do not want to feel abnormal. And we often do this in the absence of hard data. Hence, many sketchy business practices take place because people feel that "everybody does it." For example, Aaron Beam, the former CFO of HealthSouth (discussed in Chapter 3) described his thoughts about earnings manipulation as follows: "You kinda assumed everybody did those kinds of things, people managed their earnings. I grew up in the era where that was an actual term, 'managing earnings.' I thought of it like that, and not being fraudulent."[9]

The Emperor Has No Clothes

Misperceiving norms doesn't always mean we think of our behavior as common or believe we are in the majority. Sometimes people are afraid to speak up because they think they're in the minority. And when silent majorities lose out, these misperceptions can become self-fulfilling prophecies.

People have known about this phenomenon for a long time. Do you remember the story "The Emperor's New Clothes" by Hans Christian Andersen? Two conmen posing as master weavers offer to craft a magical set of garments for the Emperor. These clothes will be beautiful to behold, but only to people who deserve their station in society. To those who are stupid or unfit for their jobs, the clothes will be invisible. The emperor hires the weavers, who pretend to outfit him with a set of garments that don't actually exist, thus leaving him naked.

When the emperor appears before his subjects in his birthday suit, no one dares challenge his authority. People privately think the emperor is naked, but they second guess themselves, and they don't want to say he's naked, lest others conclude that they are stupid and unfit for their jobs. It takes a small boy in the crowd to cry out "But he isn't wearing anything at all!" before everyone else is able to speak the truth.

Psychologists have a term for this: *pluralistic ignorance.*[10] It occurs when people misrepresent their private beliefs because they perceive them to be uncommon or unpopular. Pluralistic ignorance can arise whenever individuals come to inaccurate conclusions about each other's beliefs, based on a consistent pattern of public behavior that doesn't accurately reflect those beliefs.

Note that pluralistic ignorance is in some sense the opposite of the false consensus effect. False consensus arises when people mistakenly overestimate how much others *agree* with them, whereas pluralistic ignorance arises when people mistakenly overestimate how much others *disagree* with them.

When should we expect each effect to arise? The answer depends on the "data" that we get about others' beliefs. False consensus is more likely when we don't observe any public expression of other people's beliefs or when we observe varying patterns of behavior, with some people doing one thing and others doing the opposite. In these cases, we tend to perceive the ambiguous data as indicating that our own beliefs are common. Pluralistic ignorance, in contrast, is more likely when there is social pressure to conform to a uniform norm of public behavior that diverges from what people believe and do in private. If this divergence is severe and people mistakenly think others' public actions reflect their privately held values, it's possible to have a silent majority that doesn't realize they're in the majority.

We've all seen versions of pluralistic ignorance in our daily lives. For instance, often there is silence when a teacher asks "Any questions?" at the end of a lecture. In our own experience, both as students and now as professors, we have seen situations where several students have questions, but they observe the initial silence and assume their peers understood the lecture. Being afraid to appear ignorant, and mistakenly thinking nobody else is confused, they keep their hands down as well.

For companies, pluralistic ignorance is a problem because it can reinforce norms that are out of step with people's personal values and that aren't even in the best interest of the firm. For example, in many elite organizations, people are expected to be at the office late into the night and even when they are on vacation they are expected to be constantly available and thinking about work. This sort of norm can create misery for individual employees and their families. It's not always good for the firm either: Although there are times when an intense spurt of effort is necessary to complete an urgent project, nonstop maximal effort burns employees out and makes them less productive. But the norm is nonetheless stable and employees might not even realize that their coworkers don't buy into it. Even employees who don't like the norm have a tendency to reinforce it with their own behavior by keeping the lights on in their office as they work late and by sending emails in the middle of the night or on weekends.

Perhaps the most common way that pluralistic ignorance arises in organizations is when discussions are dominated by the views of a small minority so that opposing, widely popular viewpoints never get raised. This is a key factor that can cause an organization to make a bad decision or take an unethical course of action: A silent majority has a sense that something is wrong, but if they think their opinions aren't widely shared, they are reluctant to voice dissent.

CASE STUDIES OF THE POWER OF THE SITUATION

We now turn to two case studies that show the negative as well as positive effects of situational factors.

Rigging the LIBOR

The London Interbank Offered Rate (LIBOR) is a benchmark for financial transactions around the world, including interest rates for mortgages, credit cards, and student loans. The LIBOR is based on a group of banks' estimates of the rates they pay for short-term loans from other banks.

Those same banks also have derivatives traders whose profits or losses depend on LIBOR rates. Derivatives and the LIBOR are somewhat technically complicated, but for our purposes the key thing to know is that derivatives traders can gain or lose quite a bit of money based on what LIBOR turns out to be, which is calculated using the supposedly honest estimates their banks submit.

Starting in 2012, it was revealed that bankers at several institutions, including Barclays, RBS, UBS, Deutsche Bank, Citigroup, JP Morgan, HSBC, and Bank of America had been manipulating the LIBOR and other baseline rates such as the Euribor, Yen LIBOR, and foreign exchange rates, often in collusion across banks. Collectively, the banks wound up paying billions of dollars in fines for their misconduct.[11]

It's easy to see this as a simple case of corporate greed, and there definitely was greed involved. But a more nuanced approach is to think of banks as organizations rather than monoliths, and to consider what was going on inside them, focusing on the role of status, conformity, and perceptions of social norms.

Within a bank, the high-flying traders were the ones who took big risks, made big money, and had high status. The people who submitted rates for calculation of the LIBOR, in contrast, had boring back-end jobs, maintaining the bank's liquidity in various currencies. The power differential often showed up in their interactions with each other. For example, one rate submitter responded to a trader's request for LIBOR manipulation by saying "Always happy to help, leave it with me, Sir." Another was more colorful: "Done ... for you big boy ... ." At a few banks, the submitters and traders were located in the same office, even at adjacent desks, a setup that undoubtedly made it harder for submitters to resist pressure to manipulate the rates.

Although many derivatives traders never attempted to manipulate rates, among those who did, rate-rigging came to feel like a completely normal practice. Reflecting on the scandal, a former trader at Morgan Stanley described how early in his career "I talked with some of my more experienced colleagues about this. They told me banks misreported the LIBOR rates in a way that would generally bring them profits. I had been unaware of that, as I was relatively new to financial trading. My naivety seemed to be humorous to my colleagues." Many traders who asked for rate manipulation didn't even make a serious attempt to hide what they were doing. One of them wrote to a rate submitter "when I retire and write a book about this business your name will be written in golden letters," to which the submitter responded "I would prefer this [to] not be in any book!" It was easy for prosecutors to build their cases against the riggers because so many of the crimes were openly discussed by text and email. This wasn't a grand conspiracy of criminal masterminds, but rather a set of people who normalized unethical and illegal behavior as commonplace.

How could institutions have been designed differently to avoid LIBOR manipulation? One possibility would be to reduce the opportunity for manipulation by basing rates on actual transactions rather than estimates provided by experts in a bank. In fact, this reform was implemented in the Secured Overnight Funding Rate (SOFR), a new rate designed to replace the LIBOR.

Another possibility is the establishment of informational firewalls to mitigate conflicts of interest by prohibiting the sharing of information across different subunits of a company. For instance, in investment banks, communication between individuals with conflicts of interest (traders, mergers and acquisitions bankers, research analysts) is restricted, and they are placed on different floors with restricted access to each other's physical spaces. One would have to actively attempt to obtain information improperly, rather than casually obtain it by visiting a friend on a different floor.

The Montgomery Bus Boycott

Many stories of the US civil rights movement focus on the heroism of individual leaders like Rosa Parks and Martin Luther King, Jr. But the movement also required a tremendous amount of organization and commitment by less-famous people, who worked tirelessly and put themselves at risk of being arrested, beaten, or killed for their actions. Their commitment was made possible by social influence and authority. Much of the authority came from the Black church, where ministers and other leaders laid out the path for their congregants to follow.

Even the leaders used the support of others as a resource. Although Rosa Parks was alone at the moment in November 1955 when she courageously refused to move to the back of the bus in Montgomery, Alabama, she had years of experience as an activist in the NAACP. In fact, earlier in 1955, after a 15-year-old girl, Claudette Colvin, had been arrested for refusing to go to the back of the bus, Parks and other local leaders met with city and bus company officials to try to convince them to change policies on segregation. Their efforts were rebuffed, but Rosa Parks knew she had the support of those around her. She also had trained in civil disobedience at the Highlander Folk School, so she was prepared for the situations she would encounter when she was arrested.[12]

The boycott following Parks's arrest was organized by dozens of community organizations, including the Montgomery Improvement Association, led by a not-yet-famous Martin Luther King, Jr., and the Women's Political Council, led by Jo Ann Robinson. Years later, describing the start of the boycott, Robinson said "It was a spontaneous act from those persons who were not members of the Women's Political Council. But we had worked for at least three years getting that thing organized ... I as President of the main body of the Women's Political Council got on the phone and I called all the officers of the three chapters. I called as many of the men who had supported us as possible and I told them that Rosa Parks had been arrested and she would be tried. They said, you have the plans, put them into operation. I called every person who was in every school and everyplace where we had planned to be ... have somebody at that school or wherever it was at a certain time that I would be there with materials for them to disseminate. I didn't go to bed that night. I cut those stencils [for handbills]. I ran off 35,000 copies."[13]

The civil rights organizations succeeded in dramatically shifting norms, so that 90 percent of Black people in Montgomery refrained from taking the bus, even though they had to go through great inconvenience as they walked or carpooled to and from work every day for months on end. With a new social norm established, the Black community kept the boycott going strong for a full year, until the Supreme Court ordered the city to integrate the busses.

STRATEGIES FOR ORGANIZATIONAL DESIGN

Given that norms, social influence, and authority can powerfully shape people's behavior, either for good or for ill, a key question is how to design institutions that will channel these forces in the right direction. Each organization faces unique challenges, but we'll present some general principles and suggestions.

First, think hard about how your organization makes decisions and whether your processes allow misperceptions to take hold. Do you have processes in place that encourage dissent and ensure that bad ideas – even those that initially seem to have a lot of support – get shot down? Or do your procedures allow for groupthink? To surface all of the relevant information in a group, it's crucial that the process be one that allows for, and even encourages, nonconformity.

One way to reduce conformity in a meeting is to take straw polls or have people jot down their thoughts individually, before the discussion begins. In our class at the Stanford GSB, we do a variant of this, polling students anonymously before starting some of our case discussions. Our students are often quite surprised by how much they disagree with each other, and by how much support even minority views have.

Another approach is to solicit comments in order of reverse seniority. In many organizations, senior managers speak first, and then junior employees simply parrot these opinions to stay in the good graces of their bosses. This is not a good approach for manufacturing dissent. In contrast, if junior employees are asked to speak first, they may raise concerns that were not on the organization's radar screen.

Organizations should also think about creating "devil's advocate" roles and assigning people the job of trying to shoot down ideas. This can ensure rigorous vetting of proposals before decisions are made. This approach detaches the individual from the argument, so that people aren't punished for being "negative Nellies" who are not team players. If the devil's advocate role rotates among group members, and there are high expectations for doing a good job as a devil's advocate, then careful consideration of dissenting arguments can be institutionalized. Good ideas should be able to survive the gauntlet of getting past a devil's advocate tasked with doing everything they can to raise serious concerns and objections.

What other institutional solutions can be used to encourage dissent? Recall that in the Milgram experiment the compliance rate plummeted when people knew they were not alone. They were much more likely to stand up to authority figures when they knew others were on their side. To help facilitate this sort of collective action, law school professors Ian Ayres and Cait Unkovic developed a concept known as the "information escrow."[14] Originally designed to combat sexual harassment and abuse, the information escrow can be used in any setting where employees may find it difficult to raise concerns about misbehavior. In an information escrow system, if someone has a complaint, they can register it online with a date stamp. They can choose to have the complaint remain anonymous and sealed in the escrow. If someone else reports a similar issue, everyone who has submitted a report is told that there are multiple reports of misconduct, and they can decide how to proceed, including by joining together to express their concerns collectively. The fact that the reports were initially made independently, as well as the fact that they were date-stamped, increases their credibility and power.

Another important factor is how an organization's top leaders respond to reports of problems. If they listen and react constructively to concerns that an organization isn't living up to its values, then everyone sees that the values are real. But if the reports are ignored or if there is retaliation against people who raise concerns, others will learn not to raise issues. This can become a self-perpetuating cycle as people see that nobody else is standing up, and everyone realizes that the organization's so-called values are actually a sham. That's the sort of situation that can lead to a major scandal. As painful as it can be for leaders to take steps to address problems, it's much worse if a problem festers, harming employees or other stakeholders along the way, and ultimately blowing up in public.

Overall, our recommendation is not to rely on the innate goodness of people in your organization, but rather to help them out by setting up situations that help them live up to their values. It's not enough to set up institutions in which it is *possible* for people to do the right thing. Rather, we need to set up institutions where they are *actively encouraged* to do it.

STRATEGIES FOR INDIVIDUAL DECISIONS

The same basic observation applies to our own individual choices. Most of us think we're pretty good people, and we think our own innate goodness ensures that we'll do the right thing pretty much all the time. We fail to anticipate how strongly our future behavior will be influenced by the situations we encounter.

This means that if you're going into a situation where you might be pressured to do something out of step with your values, it's not a good idea to just assume you'll do the right thing. You also need a *plan*. Of course, your exact plan should depend on the nature of the situation as well as your own personal values and commitments. But at the very least, you should be able to answer questions like "When my business partner, boss, customer, or friend asks me to do X, how will I say no?"

In the moment, many people find it surprisingly difficult to say no to things that are clearly against their values. Thus, an important and generally useful tactic is to get yourself out of the immediate context where pressure is being put on you. Distance from the people who are pressuring you can reduce their power. Buying yourself time is also useful. If you have time to reflect on a decision and how it relates to your core values, you are less likely to be like the seminary students who failed to help a man in distress as they hurried to give a speech about The Good Samaritan.

Given the power of conformity and social pressures, it's also important to realize that if you have objections, others may agree with you but not yet feel comfortable expressing their views openly. An important form of leadership is to take a stand, not knowing for sure that others will join, but hoping they will.

More generally, it's a good idea to avoid putting yourself in difficult situations in the first place. It's easy to think that we'll maintain our virtue and character no matter the circumstances. After all, that's what heroes do. But the most important lesson of social psychology is that this confidence in ourselves is misplaced. The way to do good is not just by being a good person but also by putting ourselves in situations that bring out the best in us, not the worst.

This is true for every life decision we make: the jobs we take, the positions we accept, the business partners we work with, the religious or community organizations we join, the people we marry, and the friends we hang out with. They all shape who we become.

WHERE DO WE GO FROM HERE?

You might have noticed that many of the concepts we have described so far in this book are scientific phenomena without values attached to them. For instance, this chapter has analyzed social influence. This can be framed negatively as conformity, but it can also be framed positively as a key part of teamwork. The workers at the NUMMI plant were influenced by social norms, but in a positive way as they worked together as a team in pursuit of a common purpose. We've also discussed the concept of authority with respect to the Milgram experiment. This can be negatively framed as obedience, but we can also think about it positively in terms of leadership. Many great things have been accomplished because of social influence and moral leadership. Civil rights activists were willing to get beaten by police officers because they knew they were not in the struggle alone. The soldiers who landed on the beaches of Normandy on D-Day did so because they were part of a team, obeying the legitimate authority and leadership of their commanding officers. People thinking of themselves solely as individuals likely wouldn't have risen to these levels of heroism.

But what about values themselves? If you're completely sure of your own core values and how they apply to different business situations, you may think the analysis so far in this book is all you need, because it gives you insight into how to design organizations and plan your life to live by your values. You wouldn't be alone in thinking this way. In their excellent book *Blind Spots*, organizational behavior scholars Max Bazerman and Ann Tenbrunsel begin with the premise that the overriding challenge business leaders face is recognizing the ethical dimensions of a decision and overcoming our various flaws that keep us from doing the right thing.

From our perspective, that's a great start, but it's not enough, because values-based leadership also requires careful analysis of values themselves. In business and in society, there are a host of tensions and conflicts about the interests of companies, individuals, and groups. What is good for some of these actors is often not good for others. The most difficult public conflicts and the most wrenching policy decisions have to do with tradeoffs between the interests of different groups: How much should current energy use be curtailed to preserve the Earth's climate for future generations? Do companies have a responsibility to alter their operations to mitigate the spread of COVID-19, protecting their workers as well as vulnerable populations like the elderly? When hiring, how should companies think about the past and current effects of racial discrimination and inequalities? Do social media companies have a responsibility to respect users' privacy and mitigate the spread of misinformation?

As people discuss and debate these issues, they don't just have different interests, they also have different values. Some people are especially concerned about consequences for economic growth, some are concerned about individual rights, and some are concerned about social justice. To engage with others who disagree with you it is crucial to understand the values they hold dear. And within our own thinking as individuals, we often bring these different concerns to bear as we think about different issues.

Our values spring from the moral intuitions that we analyzed in Chapter 2, but they also have a lot of structure and nuance. Taking our own values – and the values of others – seriously requires thinking about them rigorously and systematically. It also requires thinking carefully about the appropriate role of companies, and business leaders, in society. In the next chapter we turn to these questions.

TAKEAWAYS

1. People's moral choices are often governed by their situations and social environments. Examples of situational factors include time pressure and authority.

2. People's moral choices are driven by social norms, or the rules of behavior that govern interactions between individuals. Sometimes these social norms are explicitly stated, but often people have to infer them. Sometimes these inferences are incorrect and social norms are misperceived.

3. Social norms are misperceived in predictable ways. Two examples of misperceptions are the false consensus effect and pluralistic ignorance, both of which can lead us to take unethical actions or make bad decisions because we misperceive those actions as acceptable norms.

4. There are numerous institutional solutions we can take to combat situational pressures and misperceptions of norms. These involve collecting and providing more information about norms as well as encouraging dissent.

5. At an individual level, it is important to plan for how to approach situations where we are pressured to do things that are out of step with our values. It's also a good idea to avoid putting ourselves in those situations in the first place.

SUGGESTIONS FOR FURTHER READING

For a broad overview of the topic of social influence – not only limited to the domain of values-based leadership – we suggest Robert Cialdini's classic book *Influence*. For deeper dives into some of the case studies described in this chapter, we recommend the *This American Life* podcast episode "NUMMI" as well as David Enrich's book about the LIBOR scandal: *The Spider Network: The Wild Story of a Maths Genius and One of the Greatest Scams in Financial History*. As with the concepts in Chapter 3, as you go through the narratives, see if you can apply the various concepts from this book.

REFLECTIVE EXERCISES

1. Have you ever been in a situation where you've felt the false consensus effect or pluralistic ignorance at play?
2. Think back to the last time you ran or participated in a business meeting. Are you confident that dissenting views were able to be raised? If not, how would you change meeting procedures to avoid groupthink? How would you balance efficiency against ensuring a wide range of viewpoints?
3. One theme of this chapter is that norms can be set by company culture. How would you describe your organization's culture? Do you think it is effective at promoting values-based decision-making? If not, what sorts of reforms would you make?

5

Shareholders, Stakeholders, and Societal Institutions

This book is a remarkable human achievement. Just to be clear, we don't mean the text that we wrote. We mean the physical book itself.

Consider what is needed to produce the paper in a book. Raw material, from trees or recycling, is harvested and transported by massive vehicles to factories where a complicated set of machinery processes it and forms it into new paper. It's then shipped, using another set of vehicles, to a different factory, where it is combined with inks and glues (each of which has its own complicated supply chain) into a book. The book then goes through a multi-stage distribution chain, involving a combination of trucks, planes, warehouses, and stores, ultimately winding up in the hands of the reader. Each stage of this process runs on energy from oil, gas, and electricity, which are produced and delivered by a vast industrial infrastructure.

For an electronic version of the book, the process is even more complicated, involving a multitude of computers and servers that transmit a series of 1's and 0's and translate them into the text that you see on the screen of your computer or phone. These astonishing, electronic machines are themselves assembled from thousands of subcomponents, drawing on raw materials from around the world.

There's nothing unique about books.[1] Any industrial product requires a complicated set of capital investments, along with the effort of thousands or millions of people from all over the world who contribute in some small way to its production and distribution. Nobody involved in this process has met more than a tiny fraction of the other people.

A millennium ago, books were rare and valuable, the possessions of an elite group that included emperors, wealthy merchants, and religious authorities. People back then would have found it inconceivable that an ordinary person could buy a book, read it once or twice, and then dispose of it. And just a few decades ago, the idea that one could instantly acquire a book transmitted via wires and electromagnetic fields would have struck people as a magical fantasy.

The magic that makes all this possible is a uniquely human creation. This is most obvious for the technology involved – the machines, vehicles, factories, and computers. But it is every bit as true for the social organization that coordinates the process of developing this technology and deploying it for production. We humans are unique among animals, in that we constantly engage in large-scale cooperation with members of our own species, including those who aren't related to us and who live hundreds or thousands of miles away.

We also are unique in that we design institutions that make this cooperation possible. This includes legal institutions like contracts and property rights that undergird economic exchange. It includes political institutions, ranging from local governments to national ones to international bodies like the World Trade Organization (WTO). And it includes businesses that engage in economic activity, ranging from small local stores to enormous multinational firms.

One form of economic organization is particularly noteworthy: The corporation, which has come to play a dominant role in the modern economy. Corporations are sort of familiar to us, because they include the largest publicly held companies, including (as of 2020) tech giants Apple, Microsoft, Amazon, Alphabet (Google), Facebook, Tencent, and Alibaba, along with Berkshire Hathaway, Visa, and Johnson & Johnson.

But the superficial familiarity of corporate names may blind us to the fact that a corporation is a strange animal, one that is a not-at-all-obvious way to organize economic activity. As a legal entity, a corporation is distinct from the people, machines, and buildings that comprise it – and it can outlive all of them. This is a key reason that corporations are powerful drivers of economic growth. They facilitate cooperation and risk-taking by pooling together the capital of many for a common purpose while shielding the individual shareholders from legal liability. The earliest corporations included the Dutch and British East India Companies, which achieved vast wealth and power through monopolization and brutal colonialism. Later, corporations played a central role in economic development, the growth of industry, the globalization of production, and the digital revolution.

The first striking feature of a corporation is separation of ownership and management. People who invest in a corporation own shares in it, but this form of ownership is different than owning a house, a car, or a small business. Shareholders play no role in the corporation's day-to-day operation and only have an indirect voice, via the board of directors, on a few high-level decisions. The second key feature is limited liability, so that if the company loses money, the shareholders are not liable for the losses. The third key feature is that shares in the company are tradeable. The final, and most unusual, feature is that the corporation exists as a legal entity separate from both its shareholders and its executives. It has been granted many of the same legal rights as an individual person: It can sign contracts, file lawsuits, and be sued in court. In the United States, the Supreme Court has also established a doctrine of "corporate personhood," giving companies free speech rights as well as the right to spend money on advertisements to influence elections.

Society has granted corporations a wide array of rights. The question for this chapter is whether, along with these rights, corporations have responsibilities to society.

For individual people, we have a sense of their rights and responsibilities. When we dive into normative ethics in Chapters 6–8, we'll discuss consequences, motives, and fairness, all of which are clearly relevant ethical considerations for regular people.

But what about corporations? What is business's appropriate role in society? Should a company just care about shareholders, or should it also care about broader sets of stakeholders like customers, employees, suppliers, and the communities where it does business? What values should a company embody? And how should it act on them?

EXTERNALITIES: POSITIVE AND NEGATIVE

As a starting point, let's think about the effects that corporations have on society. In the eyes of many people, these effects can be highly negative. Corporations are often criticized in the media, movies, and popular culture. And although certain brands are popular, many people see corporations in general as being deeply problematic. For example, Gallup surveys between 2010 and 2020 consistently found that around 60 percent of Americans were either "somewhat dissatisfied" or "very dissatisfied" with "the size and influence of major corporations."[2]

It's easy to think of specific harms that corporations impose on society. Banks and investment companies precipitated a financial crisis and global recession in 2008 by ignoring the systemic risks created by their actions. Oil companies, automakers, airlines, and meat producers contribute a substantial share of the emissions that cause climate change. Massive retailers drive local stores out of business. And tech companies that dominate the flow of information seek to maximize advertising revenue and user engagement, even if that means providing a platform for false claims and malicious attempts to sway elections or undermine political systems. These are examples of *negative externalities*, that is, the ways that a company's actions harm others in society.

But it's crucial to recognize that corporations also have massive positive effects. Many of these positive effects are direct benefits for those who engage in voluntary economic transactions with a company: The person who deposits money in a bank or takes out a loan to buy a house; the consumer who uses gasoline, drives a car, takes a flight, or buys products from a retailer; and the person who uses the Internet for information and communication. The benefits of voluntary, self-interested economic exchange were recognized by the great economist Adam Smith, who stated: "It is not from the benevolence of the butcher, the brewer, or the baker that we expect our dinner, but from their regard to their own self-interest. We address ourselves, not to their humanity but to their self-love, and never talk to them of our necessities but of their advantages."[3] Or, in the language of modern business, a voluntary transaction is a *win-win* that benefits both of the parties involved. The people around the world who cooperated to make this book didn't do so because they liked each other – many of them have never even met. They cooperated because they wanted to make money.

Smith went farther than this. He didn't just say that businesses benefit those who interact directly with them. He also said that as they try to make money, an *invisible hand* guides them to do things that are beneficial for society as a whole. In other words, businesses create *positive externalities*. For a modern corporation, there are a host of these externalities. When a bank makes a loan, that's great for the proud new homeowner. And it also benefits everyone who got a job building the house. A passenger who takes a flight for a vacation isn't the only person who benefits. So do all of the people who work in the hotels, restaurants, and stores in the town that the vacationer is visiting. When consumers shop at large retailers, they save time and money, which is also good for suppliers of additional goods these consumers can afford to buy. And as an individual uses the infrastructure developed by tech companies to work from home during the era of COVID-19, they aren't the only one who benefits.

So does the rest of society, which benefits from the social distancing facilitated by stay-at-home work policies. Much of what corporations do isn't just a win-win transaction with an employee, supplier, or customer. It's a *win-win-win* that also benefits third parties and society more broadly.

Given that corporations have a variety of impacts, both positive and negative, how should business leaders think about their role in society?

MILTON FRIEDMAN'S ARGUMENT

The most famous answer to the question of corporations' role in society was given by the libertarian economist Milton Friedman in a 1970 *New York Times* article boldly entitled "The Social Responsibility of Business is to Increase Its Profits."[4] Friedman argued that corporations should give no consideration to how their actions affect others in society. They should instead "make as much money as possible while conforming to [the] basic rules of the society, both those embodied in law and those embodied in ethical custom." He argued that a company should not care about "providing employment, eliminating discrimination, avoiding pollution and whatever else may be the catchwords of the contemporary crop of reformers."

To many people, Friedman's position encapsulates everything that is wrong with the modern corporation: It is a selfish machine, solely focused on making money. Friedman's view clashes strongly with most people's intuition (which we discussed in Chapter 2) that companies can do right and wrong, and thus are morally responsible for their actions.

On the other hand, many people in business, and in business schools, talk about the responsibilities of companies in ways that closely hew to Friedman's prescription, arguing that managers and executives have an ethical responsibility to focus on only one objective: maximizing long-run value for their shareholders.

So, let's delve into the argument that Friedman made in support of his controversial conclusion about the social responsibility of business. The argument is based on a number of assumptions, about how companies are organized and about how societies function.

Friedman first makes a set of assumptions about the objectives and organization of a corporation. He begins his argument by noting that a corporation's executives are not its owners. They may be compensated heavily in stock, but ultimately they work for the shareholders. So, in Friedman's view, it is their responsibility to do what the shareholders want. Investors obviously want the firm to make money. Of course, Friedman recognizes that individual investors may care about other things too, but he notes that they typically disagree about those other objectives. Some care about the environment, others care about educational opportunities for disadvantaged children, others want to support the symphony, and others don't care about any of these things. The one thing they all agree on is that they'd like more money, so Friedman concludes that's what the firm should focus on. If some investors want to take their share of the profits and use it for other purposes, including social causes, that's fine and good, but that's a decision that they can freely make on their own. In Friedman's view, if the firm's managers sacrifice any profits in order to do good for society, they are illegitimately stealing money from investors.

Of course, there are lots of things that need to be done for society, but in Friedman's view it is not a corporation's role to do those things. Rather, it is the role of the government, and Friedman makes a second set of assumptions, about how governments and societies function. In his view, it's the government's job to set the laws that determine what companies are, and are not, allowed to do as they conduct their business. It's also the government's job to levy taxes and use the revenue to pursue social objectives. In making these decisions, the government has legitimacy, *if* it's acting in accordance with the wishes of the people, and within constitutional limits on its powers. As we will argue below, that's a pretty big "if."

In our view, a necessary condition for market capitalism to benefit society as a whole is that the government does a good job of setting public policy and regulating firms' conduct. What do such government policies look like? At a general level, they involve penalizing or prohibiting actions that create negative externalities, while subsidizing or mandating actions that create positive externalities. In the language of economics, a key role of governments is to correct *market failures*, that is, situations where profit maximizing behavior by companies can lead to bad outcomes for society.

As a simple example, suppose a company called Dinco is building a factory that will produce a lot of noise, thereby irritating nearby residents and reducing the value of their property. But suppose the noise isn't inevitable, because Dinco can purchase quieter equipment and install sound insulation in its factory. The government could calculate the costs and benefits of noise abatement and decide whether to mandate it. Alternatively, the government could tax Dinco for each decibel of noise above some predetermined level. If the tax is set equal to the harm to the neighbors' happiness and property values, then as Dinco's leaders maximize the company's profits, they will either adopt the noise-abating technology (if it is cost-effective) or compensate the government, and indirectly the neighbors, for the harms (if the technology is not cost-effective). With guidance from appropriate public policy to correct for market failures, the invisible hand can work pretty well, even in the presence of externalities.

But what if the government doesn't do such a great job of policy making (e.g., does not clearly assign the property right of a quiet neighborhood to the residents), and there are no regulations or penalties to deter Dinco from building a noisy factory? Milton Friedman would say that even if the noise abatement technology is effective and inexpensive, Dinco's executives shouldn't spend any money on it, because their duty is to maximize profits for their shareholders, not to be concerned about the neighbors or society at large.

CRITIQUES OF FRIEDMAN

As you might expect, many parts of Friedman's argument have been criticized over the past fifty years. Here we will focus on two parts of his argument: His assumptions about what shareholders want and how governments work.

Socially Responsible Investors

One critique of Friedman grants his assumption that corporations should only serve their shareholders but argues that this means considering shareholders' preferences more broadly, rather than adopting a narrow focus on profits, earnings, or share prices.

In our example of the noisy factory, it's reasonable to believe that some of Dinco's shareholders don't want to make the neighbors miserable. Suppose some of the shareholders are willing to give up 5 cents of value per share to avoid inflicting noise on the neighbors, most are willing to sacrifice 2 cents, and a few aren't willing to sacrifice anything. Why should this final group get to decide how Dinco is run? It's hard to say that the company is pursuing the interests of the shareholders if it makes decisions solely based on the preferences of the shareholders who are *least* concerned about the well-being of others in society. But that's exactly what Friedman says Dinco should do.

Moreover, shareholders are free to choose whether to invest in a company. So, if a company is forthright about the fact that it cares about broader stakeholder interests and is willing to sacrifice some profits, shareholders who are unhappy about this can simply invest their money elsewhere. Describing his company's social responsibility initiatives, Howard Schultz, the former chairman of Starbucks said, "If Friedman had balked, asserting that Starbucks could have performed even better without these 'socially responsible' activities, I would have told him what I told an institutional investor who wanted me to slash health care costs during the Great Recession, or what I said to a shareholder in 2013 who falsely claimed that Starbucks's support of gay rights hurt profits: If you feel you can get a better return elsewhere, you are free to sell your shares."[5]

Economists Oliver Hart and Luigi Zingales have argued that because some shareholders value things other than profits and all shareholders are free to choose where to invest their money, "serving shareholders doesn't mean putting profit above all else."[6] And political economist David Baron has developed models of corporate social responsibility (CSR) in which investors choose to buy shares in companies founded by social entrepreneurs.[7] The logic of these arguments is compelling, and you may find them appealing if you think corporations shouldn't be narrowly focused on maximizing financial returns for their investors.

But if that's your reaction it's also important to think carefully about what "serving shareholders" implies, and whether it actually implies a broad vision of social responsibility. In a country like the United States that has massive wealth inequality, the overwhelming majority of shares in publicly held companies are owned by the rich. Not just the rich, but the ultra-rich. Measuring wealth can be tricky, but according to the Federal Reserve, as of early 2020, the richest 1 percent of Americans had over $11 trillion invested in corporate equities and mutual funds, the next 9 percent had a bit over $8 trillion, the next 40 percent had a bit under $3 trillion, and the bottom 50 percent had essentially no equity investments.[8] The top 1 percent literally holds as much stock as everyone else combined. So, if corporations' responsibility is to serve their shareholders, they should be almost exclusively responsive to the wishes of the economic elite. The ultra-rich are sometimes generous, but often they aren't. And on many important issues their values, interests, and concerns diverge substantially from those of their fellow citizens. If corporations are to serve their shareholders, their responsibility isn't to society as a whole, but rather to high society.

Lobbying and Political Failure

Friedman's assumptions about public policy and government decision making strike most political scientists, including the authors of this book, as being wildly optimistic. In his 1970 article, he says firms shouldn't step in to address problems unaddressed by the government, because the fact that the government didn't do anything about a problem indicates that those in favor of government action "have failed to persuade a majority of their fellow citizens to be of like mind."

If governments always responded effectively to the interests and preferences of the majority of their citizens by adopting well-designed policies, then Friedman would have a good point here. But just as there are many types of market failure – monopoly power, externalities, and so on – that can cause bad outcomes for society, there also are many types of *political failure* that can cause public policy to diverge from the interests of citizens. Here are a few examples:

- Voters often lack information about what policies serve their interests, and even when they are well informed, they find it difficult to hold elected officials accountable for their actions.
- Elected officials and appointed bureaucrats often lack the information or resources necessary to design good policies and implement them effectively. For example, banking regulators are at an enormous informational disadvantage relative to the financial services industry.[9]
- Political institutions are designed to be unwieldy, and to set up obstacles in the way of government action. This can include institutions that privilege the views of a minority of citizens above the majority, such as the US Senate. The US Constitution was carefully crafted to prevent tyranny by separating powers among different parts of the government. So far, it's done a pretty good job on that front, but the design of the institutions also makes it difficult for the government to take action, especially on urgent matters.

Moreover, companies are not just neutral observers of political failure – they often contribute to it. This is most obvious when companies engage in illegal corruption, paying off politicians, or bribing bureaucrats to do their bidding. But corporations also can contribute to political failure through purely legal means, such as lobbying government officials, contributing to electoral campaigns, running advertisements in support of their preferred candidates, and drafting legislation that serves their interests. For instance, many people criticized the Energy Policy Act of 2005 as overweighting the interests of energy companies at the expense of consumer and environmental groups, who did not have equal access to the White House's Energy Task Force. The resulting legislation exempted the hydraulic fracturing ("fracking") industry from the Clean Air Act and the Clean Water Act. Similarly, after the California legislature passed a law requiring that many contract workers receive full employee protections, five companies that were heavily reliant on contract work – Uber, Lyft, Instacart, Postmates, and DoorDash – spent over $200 million to convince voters to pass a ballot initiative overturning the law.[10]

If corporations are just one of many interest groups that attempt to influence public policy, and there are other equally powerful groups that represent a broad range of competing interests, then corporate political activity isn't much of a problem. Political scientists use the term *pluralism* to describe this sort of situation, and they generally come to optimistic conclusions about how government will function under pluralism.

But often the interest group environment is asymmetric, and the competition is not evenly balanced. Each year, around $3 billion is spent on lobbying the US federal government, and all of the top spenders are business interests, including the Chamber of Commerce, realtors, pharmaceutical companies, hospitals, doctors, health insurers, tech companies, aerospace companies, and defense contractors.[11] In the European Union, participation is more balanced but still asymmetric, with business interests spending more and deploying more lobbyists than NGOs, labor unions, and civil society organizations.[12] One reason for this power asymmetry is that it is difficult for large groups of citizens to organize and much easier for a small group of corporations to coordinate with one another. Also, corporations and businesses have what political scientists call "structural power" – unlike most regular citizens, they can threaten to leave a jurisdiction if they don't get what they want from policymakers.

In the view of many people, all of this corporate lobbying is corrupt, involving an explicit or implicit quid pro quo. Others disagree and say that companies play a productive role by providing information to policymakers and helping them craft good public policy. However, political economists Alex Hirsch and Ken Shotts have shown that even under the most optimistic interpretation – in which lobbying consists solely of working to improve the quality of policy options that a company favors, without any of the corruption or deception that most people associate with lobbying – a well-resourced interest group is able to skew public policy in its favor and provide very little benefit to the general public, unless it is counterbalanced by opposing interests or civil servants who don't buy into its policy agenda.[13]

Under Friedman's reasoning, corporations – whose responsibility is to make money for their shareholders – should take advantage of political failures, just as they should take advantage of market failures. If a company can convince a government to enact a policy that makes money for its shareholders despite causing harm to the rest of society, that's fine, as long as the company doesn't engage in corruption or other illegal activity.

But then the other part of Friedman's argument falls apart, because public policy doesn't reflect the will of the people, but rather the will of powerful corporations. In our example of Dinco's noisy factory, it's one thing if the government responds to its citizens' wishes when it decides not to regulate or fine the company. It's quite another matter if the government's policy is drafted by Dinco's lobbyists and enacted by politicians who expect to receive support from Dinco when they're up for reelection.

EVOLVING NOTIONS OF CORPORATE SOCIAL RESPONSIBILITY

In the years since Friedman penned his essay, there have been major shifts in thinking about corporations' responsibilities to society. In the 1970s and 1980s, his argument gained a lot of traction at business schools and among executives, like Jack Welch, the former Chairman and CEO of General Electric. In 1981, Welch gave a famous speech at The Pierre Hotel in New York City, in which he argued that the stagnant economy was partially due to the failure of executives to drive value for their shareholders. In many ways, the primacy of shareholder value was originally a positive thing, focused on ensuring the accountability and responsibility of business managers.

But in subsequent decades, the trend has gone in the opposite direction, as an increasing number of thinkers, including Rebecca Henderson, Lynn Stout, Ian Mitroff, and R. Edward Freeman, have argued in favor of stakeholder value, the idea that executives do not simply have a responsibility to shareholders, but also to other groups such as employees, customers, suppliers, and communities.[14] In this view, corporations do not exist independently of society. Rather, they are creations of society and they depend on it for everything they do, so it is reasonable for society to expect them to take a broader set of stakeholders into account. And employees, customers, civil society organizations, and activist investors have increasingly demanded that corporations do this.

The idea of stakeholder value has also gained increasing traction among business leaders. In 2018, Larry Fink, the CEO of BlackRock, the world's largest asset manager, with around $7 trillion of assets under management, got a lot of attention with his annual memo to CEOs of portfolio companies, which stated: "Society is demanding that companies, both public and private, serve a social purpose. *To prosper over time, every company must not only show that it delivers solid financial performance, but also show how it makes a positive contribution to society.* Communities must benefit all of their stakeholders, including shareholders, customers, employees, and the communities in which they operate" (*emphasis in original*).[15]

In 2019, the Business Roundtable, an association of the CEOs of the largest companies in the United States, also took a step in this direction. For decades, the Roundtable had released statements about corporate governance in which it argued that firms should pay attention to stakeholders, but only as a means of increasing long-run value for shareholders. The Roundtable's 2019 statement, however, listed shareholders as just one group among many stakeholders. The members of the Roundtable said they were committed to delivering value for all of these stakeholders, and the accompanying press release said they were moving away from shareholder primacy and adopting "a modern standard for corporate responsibility."[16]

This approach has also been articulated by individual CEOs, including Marc Benioff of Salesforce, who wrote in 2020 that Friedman's article had "brainwashed a generation of CEOs," and blamed Friedman's approach for "economic, racial and health inequalities" and "the catastrophe of climate change."[17]

One might even think there is an emerging consensus that the "ethical custom" referred to by Friedman now includes concern for the interests of stakeholders as well as shareholders. But this newfound emphasis on stakeholders raises a host of questions, some of which we will now discuss.

Is It Legal?

You might wonder whether it's legal for a company's leaders to consider the interests of anyone other than shareholders, or whether *fiduciary duty* requires them to focus solely on shareholder value. According to law professor Lynn Stout, it is legal to consider other interests, because the laws under which corporations are established allow them to pursue "any lawful business purpose."[18]

As noted by Stout, a recent Supreme Court majority opinion stated that "While it is certainly true that a central objective of for-profit corporations is to make money, modern corporate law does not require for-profit corporations to pursue profit at the expense of everything else, and many do not do so. For-profit corporations, with ownership approval, support a wide variety of charitable causes, and it is not at all uncommon for such corporations to further humanitarian and other altruistic objectives." The Court then went on to list other things companies do that diverge from the pursuit of profit, including pollution control, energy conservation, and improving working conditions abroad. You might think this was the opinion of the Court's liberal wing, but the decision was written by Justice Samuel Alito, stating the position of the conservative majority in the controversial *Hobby Lobby* case, which held that, based on their religious beliefs, the owners of a closely held company could refuse to cover contraceptive health coverage for their employees.

Not everyone agrees with the argument that corporations are free to pursue the interests of nonshareholders. Leo Strine, the then Chief Justice of the Delaware Supreme Court, wrote that according to Delaware law (under which many companies are incorporated) a board of directors "must make stockholder welfare their sole end, and that other interests may be taken into consideration only as a means of promoting stockholder welfare."[19]

We're not legal scholars, so we're not going to dive into the details of these debates. For practical purposes, the key thing to know is that regardless of their views on companies' responsibilities, legal scholars unanimously agree that corporate boards and executives have enormous discretion in the decisions they make. Under the *business judgment rule*, judges recognize that it is extremely difficult for them to discern what course of action would best serve the interests of a corporation, so they defer to the judgment of the company's leaders, except for extreme cases involving things like fraud, embezzlement, self-dealing, or gross negligence. Thus, for example, the CEOs who signed the 2019 Business Roundtable statement are not in any legal jeopardy if they take actions to benefit a broad set of stakeholders.

What about Trade-offs?

Despite recent emphasis on stakeholder value, shareholder value remains the beacon that guides most business decisions. Much of the conversation about stakeholder value has focused on win-win (or win-win-win) opportunities, the sort of things that nobody can really take issue with. For example, in an influential 2011 article in *Harvard Business Review*, Michael Porter and Mark Kramer argued that companies should focus on "creating shared value," by developing new products for underserved markets, reducing energy use, building long-term relationships with suppliers, and investing in their employees' well-being.[20] According to Porter and Kramer, this approach is better than traditional CSR, because it is linked to the core of the business and produces benefits not only for stakeholders but also, in the long run, for the firm itself. Similarly, Larry Fink's BlackRock memo said that strong long-run financial performance requires strong long-run social performance.

It's important to be clear that this sort of win-win thinking is not a fundamental repudiation of Friedman's argument. It just adds to Friedman's focus on shareholders' interests a more nuanced set of claims about *enlightened self-interest*. Friedman would wholeheartedly agree that companies ought to focus on maximizing long-run shareholder value rather than quarterly earnings or next week's share price. In fact, to do otherwise would be to fail to serve shareholders' interests! What he would be skeptical about is the notion that caring about a broad set of stakeholders is the route to long-run profitability. But that's just a question of strategy and tactics, not values and purpose.

It is in situations that are *not* win-win that values and purpose are most relevant. And critics have expressed deep skepticism about whether the Business Roundtable CEOs and other executives who espouse stakeholder capitalism will do anything other than promote their shareholders' interests when push comes to shove.

In August 2020, in the midst of the COVID-19 pandemic, Salesforce reported an extremely strong fiscal quarter. CEO Marc Benioff celebrated the company's success, saying "Salesforce was founded on our belief in stakeholder capitalism ... Our success in the quarter brought all of this together with the power of our Customer 360 platform, the resilience of our business model, putting our customers first and doing our part to take care of all of our stakeholders."[21] The quarterly report was great news for shareholders, who saw the stock price soar by 29 percent. Yet for some Salesforce employees the news wasn't so good, as the very next day the company announced that it would eliminate 1,000 jobs.[22] Salesforce wasn't alone. Many CEOs who signed the Business Roundtable statement were criticized for paying out dividends and collecting bonuses for themselves during the pandemic, while furloughing or firing low-paid workers. This prompted economist Lawrence Katz to say that "there's a lot of lip service" in the Roundtable statement.[23]

Writing in *The Washington Post*, the economist and former Treasury Secretary Larry Summers argued that if members of the Roundtable were truly committed to the well-being of stakeholders they would support government policies and regulations that benefit those stakeholders.[24] But an analysis by the Center for Political Accountability found that many companies who made pronouncements about valuing stakeholders donated to candidates and lobbying groups who supported policies that were harmful to those stakeholders.[25]

So it remains to be seen how companies and executives who have recently espoused stakeholder capitalism will behave as they make decisions that involve trade-offs between the interests of shareholders and other stakeholders.

Implementation

If the idea of stakeholder value is to have any real meaning, rather than simply being a form of virtue signaling for companies that want to make themselves look good, it has to mean that a company is sometimes willing to sacrifice long-run shareholder value. Whether your company is willing to do that is not for us to decide. But if you do decide to do it, you need to take into account five key components, which we will refer to as the 5 P's (Priorities, Performance Metrics, Pay, Promotions, and Power).

- Priorities. The company must decide how to weigh the interests of different stakeholders when they come into conflict with each other. For instance, will the company take an action that is good for employees but bad for consumers? Or good for suppliers but bad for the environment? Should the company only respond to the demands of stakeholders who are organized and influential, or should it also consider groups with little power, like the poor and the unemployed? And how much return for shareholders is the company willing to sacrifice for the benefit of various stakeholders?
- Performance Metrics. In contrast to a share price, it's often quite difficult to assess impact on stakeholders. But such measurement, as well as ongoing evaluation of the company's efforts, is crucial if a company wants to have an impact.
- Pay. In many companies, senior executives are incentivized with options or bonuses that depend on the company's share price. A company that cares about stakeholders should likewise incentivize performance on the metrics that it uses to assess impact.

- Promotions. As with pay, a company can take stakeholder performance metrics into account when making decisions about promotions.
- Power. Ultimately, the values of an organization, and what sort of
  behavior is incentivized and rewarded, depend on who holds power.
  So, a company that cares about stakeholder impact needs to actively
  select board members and senior executives who share those values.
  Employees who focus on social responsibility need to be in the C-suite,
  not siloed within peripheral offices. Organizational priorities are
  reflected in who has a seat at the table.

None of the 5 P's are easy or straightforward to implement. But neither is
anything else in an organization with thousands of employees, each of
whose actions have only a minor and highly indirect effect on the
company's performance.

Corporate structures continually evolve, and recently new institutional
forms have emerged, including benefit corporations and certified
B corporations, that are designed to provide a structure for taking stakeholder interests into account. Similarly, impact investing funds are
designed to achieve both financial and social performance. Even companies that do not adopt these particular institutional forms can include
some of their features in their governance and practices.

The long-run effect of the change in how people talk about the role of
business in society remains to be seen. Some economists are skeptical that
companies are able to act effectively in the public interest, even if they want to
do so. Milton Friedman argued that executives have no expertise at promoting
social objectives and Adam Smith wrote that "By pursuing his own interest [a
businessman] frequently promotes that of the society more effectually than
when he really intends to promote it." We think these arguments are overstated. Sure, the best way to promote the public interest is for the government
to set up well-designed policies to steer self-interested behavior by corporations in the right directions. But, unfortunately, that's not the world we live
in. So leaders of corporations are often left with the choice of either doing
nothing, or trying to take stakeholders into account, knowing that they will
make some mistakes along the way, just like all the other decisions they make
when leading complicated organizations in a rapidly changing world.

SHAPING PUBLIC POLICY AND INSTITUTIONS

Many companies' statements of their responsibilities to society focus
solely on their direct interactions with stakeholders. In our view, it is

every bit as important to think about public policies that lead companies to take actions that are beneficial for society. It's hard to take a company seriously if it says it cares about its workers, but resists public policies that benefit those workers. Or if it produces glossy brochures about its green practices, but fights tooth and nail against environmental regulations. Or if it touts its commitment to communities, but tries to weaken their ability to levy taxes and exercise regulatory authority.

Unfortunately, many discussions about stakeholder value gloss over these issues or ignore them entirely. In the 2018 BlackRock memo, the only mention of public policy was a statement that companies needed to explain their strategic reactions to a massive corporate tax cut, as well as "how major legislative or regulatory changes will affect not just next year's balance sheet, but also your long-term strategy for growth." And the 2019 Business Roundtable statement said absolutely nothing about public policy.

In our view, companies have two levels of responsibility as they engage in public policy. The first, and more direct level, has to do with *specific policy decisions*. As we said before, if pluralism is functioning well, with multiple powerful competing interests, then it's fine for companies to advocate for their preferred public policies, for example by providing policymakers with (truthful) information about the beneficial effects of those policies.

But when pluralism isn't functioning well, companies (especially those that claim to care about stakeholders) have a responsibility to only push for policies that they believe are actually beneficial for society. Of course, as shown in Chapter 3, people tend to be biased in favor of their own self-interest, so business leaders should be skeptical about their own beliefs that policies that are good for their companies are also good for society. In Chapter 6, we'll have a lot more to say about assessing consequences, but for now it's probably enough to note that at the very least, a company ought to consult with NGOs and other stakeholder groups whose interests are *not* closely aligned with the company's interests to hear what they think about different public policy options.

An open question is the extent to which corporate responsibility to stakeholders is a firm-level or an industry-level concern. At first blush, it may seem that the best approach is for firms to individually set policies based on their values. But it's hard for a company to be socially responsible when its competitors are playing by a different set of rules. Therefore, in the absence of government regulation that applies to all firms, the most realistic path to socially responsible business practices may be industry-wide initiatives.

The second, deeper, level of companies' responsibilities in the public arena has to do with the *foundational institutions of governance*, which are under threat in countries around the world. There are many causes for this, including the massive disruptions of globalization and the Great Recession, the rise of populist and nationalist politicians, and the increasing role of social media in public discourse and elections. But corporations also bear some of the blame. Some of them actively work to undermine citizens' trust in science and government experts. Others build platforms for information dissemination and then deny any responsibility as domestic zealots and foreign trolls use those platforms to spew lies and hateful rhetoric – or even to organize violent uprisings – that tear at the fabric of society. And other corporations try to reshape the rules of the political game to weaken the power of groups that don't share their political agendas, even to the point of making it more difficult for citizens to vote and participate in the political process. All of these actions undermine the effectiveness and threaten the survival of democratic institutions.

In her recent book *Reimagining Capitalism in a World on Fire*, Rebecca Henderson argues that companies have a responsibility to actively support inclusive and democratic political institutions. We wholeheartedly agree. Any company that claims to care about its stakeholders must care about the foundational institutions of society. And even a company that adopts a hardline shareholder value position in the Friedman tradition must recognize that it's unacceptable to undermine "law and ethical custom" in the society that makes the corporation's existence possible.

CASE STUDIES OF INSTITUTIONS AND INCENTIVES

We now turn to two examples of how societal institutions shape companies' incentives, as well as the roles that companies play in shaping public policy.

The Boeing 737 MAX

In 2017, aerospace giant Boeing delivered a new version of its most popular plane. Relative to previous 737s, the MAX offered improvements on several key dimensions: length, range, and fuel economy. Boeing also designed the plane to save airlines money, by minimizing the amount of expensive retraining required for current 737 pilots to fly the MAX.

Boeing quickly received thousands of orders for the new plane, which was seen as a strong competitor for Airbus's A320neo. The plane and the company seemed to be headed on an upward trajectory.

Then, in late 2018 and early 2019, two 737 MAXes crashed in Indonesia and Ethiopia, suddenly nosediving shortly after takeoff and killing a total of 346 people. Boeing initially tried to attribute the crashes solely to pilot error, but it soon became clear that the 737 MAX also had a dangerous design flaw that increased the likelihood of operator error. To increase the plane's capacity, Boeing had installed larger, more powerful engines, which could occasionally cause the plane's nose to pitch upward. To adjust for this, Boeing developed an automated Maneuvering Characteristics Augmentation System (MCAS) to push the plane's nose back down. But MCAS would occasionally make adjustments that were too severe, and unless pilots reacted within a few seconds, the plane could wind up plunging to the earth. Boeing's training materials for the 737 MAX hardly mentioned MCAS and pilots weren't provided with any warnings about it.

Following the crashes in Indonesia and Ethiopia, the 737 MAX was grounded in March 2019, first by regulators in China, then by other regulators around the world, and finally by the US Federal Aviation Administration (FAA). Boeing's stock price plunged, losing billions of dollars of market value.

The story of the 737 MAX is a clear example of the importance of prioritizing stakeholders as part of a company's strategy for long-run profitability. Boeing unambiguously failed two of its most important stakeholders – airlines and the flying public – and subsequently paid the price.

The case also illustrates the importance of societal institutions. Boeing has been sued in US federal court by dozens of families who lost loved ones in the 737 MAX crashes. In a settlement with the US Justice Department, the company paid $1.77 billion to airlines and $500 million to families of crash victims.[26] Although some businesspeople disparage the US liability system, it's important to note that it provides companies with an incentive to take precautions to prevent injury or death to customers.

At a deeper level, the case illustrates that effective functioning of societal institutions requires that companies engage with them appropriately and in good faith. The FAA allows Boeing to certify its own planes as meeting safety standards. Lacking the staff, funding, and technical resources to thoroughly assess the company's products, the FAA has instead relied on a system of self-regulation. Although there is debate as to whether the failure of the 737 MAX was due to mistakes or willful negligence, it is clear that the self-regulation system failed society.

In many ways, the scandal with the 737 MAX is the exception rather than the rule when it comes to aviation safety. Generally, self-regulation in the airline industry works well because a plane falling out of the sky is an event that's horrific, salient, and sometimes directly attributable to the corporations. In many ways, Boeing's incentives are well aligned with the government and the flying public. In other industries where self-regulation is common, there are fewer safeguards. For instance, in financial services, there's often an incentive to take on too much risk, which has negative impacts on society. As finance professor and reform advocate Anat Admati writes: "The fear of being directly responsible for deaths prevents individuals involved in maintaining safe aviation from failing to do their part. In banking, public interest in safety conflicts with the incentives of people within the industry."[27]

Climate Change

Climate change is a fundamental threat to human well-being. The science is clear: Climate change is real, it's large, it's caused by human activity, and its effects are likely to be devastating. Despite this, humans are doing far too little to head off this looming catastrophe.

The problem won't be solved by individual decisions. People around the world would all be better off if everyone reduced their CO_2 emissions. But this is a *collective action problem*, and nobody has much incentive to reduce their own personal emissions.

Nor will the problem be solved by companies' enlightened self-interest. Sure, a few companies have voluntarily reduced their emissions. But aside from making energy efficiency improvements that pay for themselves by reducing expenses, most companies don't see long-term financial benefits that justify the costs.

In the absence of government intervention, climate change isn't going to be stopped or even slowed. Fortunately, there are well-understood policies that governments can use to reduce carbon emissions. They can limit emissions with policies like fuel economy standards for cars. Or, they can adopt a more efficient policy like a cap and trade system, limiting the total amount of emissions and allowing the market to determine how to achieve reductions most efficiently. Or they can impose a carbon tax, so that companies have to internalize the harms caused by their emissions.

Many approaches could address the crisis, and none of this is rocket science.

Why doesn't it happen? In part, the reason is that, just like individual people and individual companies, individual countries have an incentive to free ride on the efforts of others. Because climate change is a global problem, many countries hope that others will bear the burden of addressing it. Further, a lot of people in developing countries feel it is unfair and hypocritical for developed nations – many of which were colonizers and all of which took advantage of carbon-based industrialization – to try to keep poorer countries from having the same opportunity to industrialize and build the middle class. Despite these tensions, many governments are nonetheless willing to make a substantial sacrifice as part of collective international efforts like the 2016 Paris Agreement.

These efforts are undermined by climate change deniers, including citizens, media figures, and politicians who claim that climate change is a "hoax." But they're not the only ones to blame: Many corporations have worked to undermine public confidence in climate science and to deny their contributions to the problem. ExxonMobil for years went against the conclusions of its own scientists, denying climate change and its human causes, while funding groups like the American Legislative Exchange Council (ALEC) and American Petroleum Institute (API) that pushed this message to legislators, the media, and the public. Meat producers fund the Center for Consumer Freedom, an astroturf (i.e., fake grassroots) organization run by a former tobacco lobbyist, which runs advertisements attacking meat alternatives and publishes opinion pieces claiming that meat production does not contribute to climate change.

No serious expert agrees with the claims made by climate change deniers. But they have succeeded in undermining public trust in experts to the point that according to surveys conducted by Pew in 2019 and 2020 only half of Americans believe that "human activity contributes a great deal to climate change." And although two thirds of Americans believe "the government is doing too little to reduce the effects of climate change," a majority of Republicans disagree.[28] This sort of atmosphere, along with lobbying and campaign contributions, sets the stage for political dysfunction and policy choices like the Trump Administration's decisions to withdraw from the Paris Agreement and roll back fuel economy standards for cars and light trucks.

Even fans of Milton Friedman's argument that companies should maximize profits subject to law and ethical custom should have serious qualms about the role that companies play in shaping climate policy.

TAKEAWAYS

1. Corporations produce enormous benefits for society, but also generate a wide range of negative externalities due to market failures.
2. Well-crafted laws and public policies can correct market failures, so that profit-maximizing behavior by companies leads to good outcomes for society.
3. One view of how companies should think about their role in society is that they should focus exclusively on shareholder value, within the boundaries set by law and ethical custom.
4. The shareholder value view has been criticized on the grounds that shareholders care about things other than profits and that political failures result in laws that serve companies rather than citizens.
5. A more recent view of how companies should think about their role in society is that they should consider stakeholder value – how their actions affect customers, employees, suppliers, and communities, not just as a means to profitability, but also as part of the company's mission.
6. Implementation of a meaningful stakeholder value approach requires the 5 P's: Priorities, Performance Metrics, Pay, Promotions, and Power.

SUGGESTIONS FOR FURTHER READING

Regardless of your position on Milton Friedman's views on CSR, you should read his 1970 *New York Times Magazine* piece "A Friedman Doctrine: The Social Responsibility of Business is to Increase Its Profits." A recent fifty-year retrospective on Friedman's piece in the *New York Times*, entitled "Greed is Good. Except When It's Bad," featured a wide range of commentary (both positive and negative) by academics and business leaders. If you're interested in win-win takes on companies' responsibilities to society we recommend Michael Porter and Mark Kramer's *Harvard Business Review* article "Creating Shared Value. How to Reinvent Capitalism – and Unleash a Wave of Innovation and Growth." As you read it, you should ask yourself: Would Friedman disagree with anything they argue? Are the opportunities for win-wins they identify ubiquitous or are they assuming away relevant trade-offs that are pervasive in the business world? Two important recent books that place more emphasis on responsibilities to external stakeholders are

Lynn A. Stout's *The Shareholder Value Myth: How Putting Shareholders First Harms Investors, Corporations, and the Public* and Rebecca Henderson's *Reimagining Capitalism in a World on Fire.*

REFLECTIVE EXERCISES

1. Consider a company where you have worked. Did the company's top leaders claim to care about a broad set of stakeholders? If so, which ones? Were those claims reflected in the company's actions, or were they empty rhetoric? If you think the company's leaders were well-intentioned, but they failed to follow through on their claims about stakeholder value, what steps should they take to align company policies with their publicly stated values?

2. What is your personal view of Friedman's argument? Should corporations always maximize shareholder value? Should they lobby for government policies that are good for shareholders, even if they are bad for others in society? If you answered "no" to either of these questions, how should they balance different stakeholder interests?

6

Weighing Consequences

As COVID-19 began to rampage through the world in the spring of 2020, societies began to ask tough questions. Should we keep stay-at-home orders in place, even though economic hardship and unemployment can lead to drug abuse and suicide? Should we maintain distance learning in schools even though it may permanently stunt child development, particularly among disadvantaged populations? Should we reopen businesses, even though doing so may cause the virus to spread and increase deaths? How do we balance the well-being of the elderly, who have the greatest risk of dying from the disease, against the well-being of children, who have their whole lives ahead of them? Others rejected the premises of these questions. Some argued that these were false choices, because the only way to have a thriving economy was to first get the virus under control. On the other side of the spectrum, some downplayed the severity of the virus altogether.

People in developed economies, many of whom were not accustomed to confronting tough choices and difficult trade-offs, suddenly faced concrete, real-life moral dilemmas with life-and-death consequences. Moreover, many of these decisions were made under the cloud of uncertainty and the difficulty of predicting complex systems. Policymakers had to act quickly, lacking precise data on how many people would become infected if a certain course of action was taken, or how much the lifetime earnings of poor children would decrease if they were unable to attend school in person for a year. In the real world, perfection could not be achieved. It would be impossible to have zero infections without shutting down a country's borders; at the same time, having tens or hundreds of millions of infections would be a disaster. These choices – made under extreme time pressure with limited information – would have massive (and differential) impacts on various groups in society.

Business leaders also faced difficult dilemmas. Because the public health situation was rapidly changing and many governments were slow to react, companies often faced tough choices about whether to go above and beyond government-established public health regulations. Manufacturers had to decide whether to shut down their factories, retailers had to decide whether to require masks and social distancing, and companies had to decide whether to implement work-from-home policies. These decisions directly affected health and economic outcomes for employees and customers. And because COVID-19 is highly contagious, the decisions made by large companies, with hundreds of thousands of employees and millions of customers, could also have a substantial effect on the severity of the pandemic in society at large.

The intense debates over how to manage COVID-19 were largely about consequences. This approach, known as *consequentialism*, is a common way people think about leading with their values. When we make decisions, we naturally consider how they will affect others. Often we want to take actions that "do no harm," a goal that is well grounded in the moral intuitions that we discussed in Chapter 2. But we also care about positive consequences, not just negative ones. For instance, many of us want a job or career in which we make a positive social impact. More broadly, some scholars, like the psychologist Joshua Greene, believe that our concern about our actions' overall impact on people's well-being is the foundational "common currency" for human morality.[1]

But what does it mean to actively promote human well-being, have a positive impact, or make the world a better place? And how does a values-based leader weigh consequences when making tough decisions? These are the questions we will address in this chapter.

Thinking about these questions rigorously and carefully is important. It's not enough to vaguely commit to "doing good." This is for two reasons. First, if we abstractly consider consequences instead of reasoning through them, we'll probably be subject to the various psychological biases covered in Chapters 2–4. We will rely too much on gut instincts, rationalize whatever actions we feel like taking (including unethical ones), and be subject to situational pressures. As we discuss later in this chapter, thinking hard about consequences does not perfectly guard against these biases. But it does discipline us into System 2 reasoning.

Second, if we don't weigh consequences carefully, we'll be tempted to falsely view everything as a "win-win." Doing this often kicks the can down the road, preventing us from confronting important trade-offs in situations where making some people better off means making others worse off. In this chapter, we'll provide a practical guide you can use to improve how you think about the consequences stemming from your and your organization's actions.

Too often in the business world, leaders talk blithely about "making a positive impact." They may identify a few benefits of their products and services without thinking seriously about potential negative consequences. This approach is very common at hot Silicon Valley startups, which tend to pitch themselves as simultaneously saving the world and making their investors rich. For instance, on Earth Day in 2016, the food delivery startup DoorDash announced that it would plant a tree for every salad purchased, and the company bragged about partnering with restaurants featuring food that was locally sourced, vegan, and organic.[2] The company didn't highlight the immense amount of plastic packaging required for food delivery, or its business model, which arguably exploits the labor of drivers and small-scale restauranteurs. Similarly, the navigation software company Waze often touted how it made the world a better place by reducing traffic congestion. This is probably true. But Waze didn't mention the negative consequences of rerouting traffic through residential neighborhoods. It is still possible that Waze does more good than harm. Yet a full consequentialist analysis explicitly takes into account all of the costs as well as the benefits.

Of course, there is an entire field of study devoted to thinking systematically about values: ethics and normative philosophy. Human beings have been trying to put structure on their moral intuitions for millennia, drawing on religion, cultural traditions, and philosophy. We'd be foolish not to draw on philosophical concepts as we develop frameworks for values-based leadership. For instance, philosophers such as Jeremy Bentham and John Stuart Mill, along with modern thinkers such as Peter Singer, have thought deeply about what it means to make decisions based on consequences. These individuals, along with others, developed the philosophy of utilitarianism, which we will draw on in this chapter.

At the same time, our goal is to give practical and actionable advice. It is therefore unhelpful to delve into the minutiae of philosophical debates. *Your* goal is to be an effective leader, not a wise philosopher. *Our* way of helping you achieve this goal is to draw upon philosophical insights and apply them to real-world leadership challenges. So, in this and the next couple of chapters we will mention philosophical concepts when needed. But we will primarily focus on the core *ideas* rather than the jargon.

CONSIDERING ALTERNATIVES

When weighing consequences, the first step is to identify the *status quo*, that is, what you or your organization are currently doing, and then lay out a broad set of alternative approaches you could adopt.

In generating alternatives, you hypothetically could consider an infinite number of possibilities, including some that are quite extreme. For instance, when deciding which of your employees to fire, you could hypothetically "fire" yourself by leaving your job, liquidating your assets and giving them to your employees, and then moving to Tibet to become a monk. In reality, the set of alternatives available to us is limited by practical considerations. For instance, we would not take a course of action that would bankrupt our company, such as giving all of our revenue to charity.

That said, people have a tendency to overly limit the set of alternatives they consider by focusing on just a couple of options, rather than a broad range of feasible possibilities. This can be problematic if the limited set of options only includes ones that we're predisposed to like, because they serve our self-interest. One key aspect of consequentialist reasoning is to think broadly and creatively about possible alternatives.

We'll provide a running example to help illustrate these ideas. In 2005, Adam Bowen and James Monsees founded a company that would eventually become Juul Labs, the largest producer of electronic cigarettes in the world. E-cigarettes present a complicated set of consequences and trade-offs. On the one hand, they seem to be much safer than traditional cigarettes and they could provide smokers a pathway to quitting. On the other hand, they are appealing to children and teenagers, and many public health advocates worry that a new generation is becoming addicted to nicotine products. Moreover, because these products are new, scientists are uncertain about the long-term health consequences of their use.

In July of 2018, Juul completed a funding round of $650 million, which valued the company at a whopping $15 billion.[3] The company was at a crossroads. It had incredible market share, partly driven by flavored products such as mint, crème brûlée, and mango. However, many public health advocates raised concerns that Juul was marketing its products to children and teenagers. Critics pointed to the flavors in Juul's product line as evidence of its nefarious marketing practices. In September 2018, the FDA sent Juul a letter giving the company sixty days to address the issue of youth vaping. The letter raised the specter of strict government regulation if the company did not police itself.

The company had to make important decisions about the design and marketing of its products – decisions with both ethical and strategic implications. The main approaches they considered involved limiting the flavors of their products and restricting the ways they were marketed. Some of the choices Juul faced were: (1) whether to advertise in media or events that had minors as a substantial share of the audience; (2) whether to advertise on social media platforms popular among minors; (3) whether to advertise near schools and playgrounds; (4) whether to use younger models in advertising campaigns; and (5) how strictly to enforce age verification requirements for retail partners.

The company also had to consider alternatives relating to its products. In addition to tobacco-flavored e-cigarettes aimed at traditional smokers, Juul also sold flavored products with sweet and fruity tastes that appealed to minors but were probably not all that appealing to older tobacco smokers. Other e-cigarette companies were much more shameless in marketing products with flavors that clearly targeted youth, with names like Unicorn Treats and Cloud Nurdz. Nonetheless, Juul needed to decide whether to continue to sell flavored products or to only sell unflavored and tobacco-flavored products.

In our consequentialist analysis of this example, we will compare the status quo to a single alternative facing Juul in 2018: Ceasing production and sale of e-cigarettes with sweet and fruity flavors. In general, we recommend considering a broad array of alternatives, but for purposes of exposition and simplicity in this example we will focus on just one.

IDENTIFYING STAKEHOLDERS

Now that we have laid out a set of alternatives, the next step in thinking like a consequentialist is to identify stakeholders who are affected by our choices. This includes customers, employees, suppliers, investors, and members of society at large – both locally and globally. As we noted in Chapter 5, stakeholders include many groups besides a company's shareholders. Values-based leaders who consider the consequences of their actions think more broadly than Milton Friedman's concept of managers as agents of shareholders.

As with laying out alternatives, people often limit themselves too much when thinking about what stakeholders to consider. The externalities from a company's actions can affect many different people in society. But, as humans, we are subject to familiarity bias, which often leads to overweighting the interests of those who are close to us. Values-based

TABLE 6.1. *A consequentialist analysis*

Comparing the Consequences of Status Quo (Selling All Flavors) to Alternative (Not Selling Flavored Products)

Stakeholders	Consequences if Juul stops selling flavored products	Net Benefits	Uncertainty
Adults who currently smoke tobacco	Less likely to adopt Juul and quit smoking	–	HIGH
Adults who currently vape	Some may quit vaping, but some may start smoking	o	HIGH
Adults who currently don't smoke or vape	Less likely to start vaping	+	HIGH
Youth who currently smoke tobacco	Less likely to adopt Juul and quit smoking	–	HIGH
Youth who currently vape	Some may quit vaping	+	HIGH
Youth who currently don't smoke or vape	Much less likely to start vaping	++	LOW
Society at large	Potentially pay higher health care costs of smokers, but lower health care costs of vapers	o	HIGH
Juul investors and employees	Lower profits	–	LOW

leaders who think about consequences try to counteract this bias and consider a very broad set of stakeholders. This can include not only people alive today, but also people who are yet to be born. For instance, many environmental sustainability initiatives are predicated on the belief that companies need to address climate change out of concern for future generations.

The first column of Table 6.1 lists the main stakeholders that could be affected if Juul decided to stop selling flavored products.

We can divide Juul's current and potential consumers into a few categories. For instance, we can separate adults from minors. This is important because there are concerns that minors are more likely to be subject to peer pressure and to get addicted. Further, there have been worries that nicotine has adverse effects on adolescent brains. Within each age cohort, we can distinguish three main groups: People who currently smoke traditional cigarettes, those who currently use e-cigarettes, and those who don't use either. These distinctions help us isolate whether product decisions will make it more likely that people will switch from e-cigarettes to traditional smoked tobacco, or whether they may start smoking. Finally, we also list two other groups of stakeholders that are nonconsumers. In the first group are members of society at large, who experience a variety of negative effects of tobacco use, ranging from sadness over illness and death of loved ones to the financial cost of providing health care. Also, we need to consider Juul itself (including its shareholders, employees, etc.) as a stakeholder because product decisions will affect the company's profitability.

COSTS AND BENEFITS

After identifying stakeholders, the next step is to determine what impact our actions will have on them compared to sticking with the status quo. Our actions could have both costs and benefits, so we must calculate the *net* benefits. Although we often employ the language of cost-benefit analysis, it's hard to know exactly what it means for something to be a cost or a benefit. Philosophers and economists therefore use the concept of *utility*. The simplest way to think of utility is that it is equivalent to happiness. But this doesn't just mean being in a good mood – rather, it refers to a deeper state of well-being or human flourishing.

One thing, among many, that affects people's utility is the amount of money that they have. The relationship between utility and income or wealth is concave. Starting from indigence, getting a bit more money initially makes a major difference in people's well-being, but eventually the curve flattens out such that each additional dollar contributes less and less to the person's happiness, as shown in Figure 6.1.

Utility is a controversial concept. There are some things people think you shouldn't put a price on – a family member's life, a rainforest full of unique species, or love for a child. However, if you want to use consequentialism to make values-based decisions, you have to put various considerations on a scale that you can use to assess trade-offs. A common way to do this is by using monetary value to compare effects across stakeholders. This may seem odd or even cold, but governments do it all the time when doing a cost-benefit analysis to decide whether to implement health and safety regulations. They calculate the value of a statistical life and determine whether the number of lives saved by a regulation is enough to justify the financial cost. It's true that every life

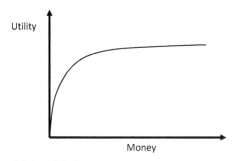

FIGURE 6.1. An additional dollar matters more to a poor person than to a rich person

is precious. However, if health and safety regulations were so onerous that every single life was preserved, the market economy as we know it would cease to function. Hence, when we think of utility, we often attempt to quantify based on monetary concerns.

Calculating net benefits often takes a lot of research, along with the requisite time and resources. When making decisions under time pressure, leaders often don't have the luxury of consulting bodies of research on costs and benefits. Further, much of this research involves untested assumptions, and it is often impossible to eliminate all uncertainty. Weighing consequences requires judgment, not just the ability to use spreadsheets.

In our Juul example, there is substantial uncertainty about many of the costs and benefits. For instance, although e-cigarettes are generally considered safer than smoked tobacco, we don't have much medical research on the long-term consequences of vaping. Some medical professionals have raised concerns that the chemicals in e-cigarettes could cause damage to people's lungs that will not be seen for decades. Accordingly, for the purposes of this exercise, we attempt to evaluate net benefits using rough categories such as very positive ("++"), positive ("+"), net zero ("o"), negative ("–"), and very negative ("– –"). The net benefits column in Table 6.1 multiplies the total number of people affected by an action by the net benefits per person. In other words, an action could be assigned a "++" if it has very positive benefits for a few people or modest benefits for a great many people.

The goal of a consequentialist analysis is to sum up the net benefits across all of the stakeholders and evaluate whether the sum is greater than or less than zero. If the summed net benefits are positive, this suggests switching from the status quo to the alternative policy. If the summed net benefits are negative, then a consequentialist analysis recommends sticking with the status quo.

When determining net benefits, there are two important things to consider. First, we need to consider both short-term and long-term effects. Because a dollar today is worth more than a dollar tomorrow, we should discount long-term effects. This is not to say that long-term benefits and costs are unimportant, only that they need to be discounted. In many cases, the long-term consequences are so severe that even when they are appropriately discounted they are still huge. Indeed, a basic human bias is to myopically focus on short-term consequences at the expense of long-term ones. This has contributed to inaction on the issue of climate change, for example.

Second, we need to appropriately take into account marginal utilities. As mentioned earlier, the relationship between money and utility is concave. So for decisions that affect people financially, it is important to consider how much marginal utility a dollar provides over what people already have. This would prioritize poorer stakeholders, who benefit from a marginal dollar much more than those who are wealthy.

In analyzing Juul's decision, let's first consider adult consumers of tobacco products (see top three rows of Table 6.1). The impact of restricting flavors is probably fairly small, because flavors are less appealing to adults. Limiting the sale of flavored products could have a small positive effect on adults who currently don't smoke or vape ("+") by making e-cigarettes less attractive. On the other hand, restricting flavors could make these e-cigarettes less attractive to traditional tobacco smokers who could potentially use them as a vehicle to quit smoked tobacco ("−"). However, given that these people are currently smoking burned tobacco, they probably are less attracted to fruity flavors in the first place. Moreover, it is unclear what the effect would be on adults who currently vape ("o"). For some individuals, removing fruity flavors could cause them to consume traditional tobacco, though this effect is probably small because they would likely be just as happy with tobacco-flavored e-cigarettes. Other individuals might abandon tobacco products altogether. Overall, Juul's decision would probably have little to no impact on adult consumers.

For youth, in contrast, Juul's decision could have substantial impact. On the one hand, restricting product choice might make the relatively safer vapes less attractive to youth who currently smoke traditional tobacco products ("−"), although tobacco-flavored products would still be available to this group. Moreover, traditional tobacco use among youth has been plummeting over the years and this group is not large to begin with. On the other hand, removing flavored products could both prevent never-vapers from becoming addicted to the product ("++") as well as encourage quitting among youth vapers ("+").

The other stakeholders are Juul, its investors, and employees, who would be worse off due to reduced profitability if Juul restricted its flavors ("−"). Given that impacts on adult tobacco smokers would most likely be limited, so too would the overall impact on the rest of society ("o").

The final column of Table 6.1 states the uncertainty associated with our utility calculations. As you can see, many of these predictions are characterized by a high degree of uncertainty, because we are making assumptions about consumer behavior for a relatively new product. A consequentialist analysis can help guide additional data collection and research on different groups to learn more about their consumption choices.

That said, the main trade-off is quite clear when we examine the line items that have low uncertainty. Limiting product offerings would hurt Juul's profits. However, it would likely lead to major benefits by preventing some young people from becoming addicted to nicotine in the first place. Further, because tobacco-flavored and unflavored products would still be available in the marketplace, Juul e-cigarettes would still be attractive products to help adult smokers quit traditional cigarettes. A consequentialist analysis would therefore argue that Juul should stop selling fruity flavors but continue to sell unflavored and tobacco-flavored products as options for current tobacco smokers who want to quit. Ultimately, under the threat of federal regulation, Juul decided in November 2018 to stop accepting retail orders for its sweet flavors but continued to sell tobacco and menthol-flavored products.[4]

RULES VS. DISCRETION

In managing organizations, we sometimes want to create a set of rules and precedents that can be followed and replicated in various situations. But we also often want the flexibility to tailor our decisions to the situation at hand. This is the age-old trade-off between rules vs. discretion, and balancing these two approaches is a key to effective leadership.

The tension between rules and discretion also crops up when it comes to weighing consequences. Philosophers distinguish between *act utilitarianism* (discretion) and *rule utilitarianism* (rules). Our analysis of Juul's dilemma is an example of an act utilitarian analysis. Juul had to make a decision about limiting products at a specific point in time. Their decision-making may have been different in a different situation characterized by different stakeholders and policy impacts. Under the logic of discretion (act utilitarianism), we want to maximize overall utility with a given action in a specific situation. Under the logic of rules (rule utilitarianism), we want to think of a set of similar situations, and then choose a rule that maximizes overall utility across the entire set of situations, especially if every company adheres to the same rule in those situations.

Whereas act utilitarianism guides a single company's choice if their goal is to maximize social welfare, rule utilitarianism helps us think of rules that all companies should follow all of the time. This means possibly choosing an action that creates net harm overall in *some* specific situations. That's the downside of rigid rules. They provide clear guidelines to follow but lead to suboptimal outcomes in some cases. On the flipside, clear standardized policies can prevent people and companies from taking actions that are overall harmful for society while deluding themselves into thinking that they're making the world a better place. (Putting constraints on discretion is also a reason to rely on government regulation rather than voluntary self-regulation by firms and industries. For example, although society would benefit if Juul stopped selling fruity vapes, the consequences would be even more positive if the government were to establish a complete ban on sweet flavors that applied to all manufacturers.)

LIMITATIONS TO CONSEQUENTIALISM

Thus far, we have argued that there are many merits to being a leader who focuses on the consequences of their actions. Our main point has been that you can be a better leader by weighing consequences carefully and analytically. However, there are limitations to consequentialism that you should be aware of. Philosophers have spent centuries debating the limitations of various values systems. Many of these debates are esoteric and don't offer practical advice for leaders. Here, we distill two key limitations that have actionable implications and should make you question the extent to which consequentialist reasoning fully embodies your core values.

One limitation to consequentialism is that it entails complexities with *measurement*.[5] People talk loosely about "impact," but if you really care about consequences then you need to assess them in a way that is reasonably accurate. Yet that can be difficult to do.

In our Juul example, you may have noticed that we sidestepped a key question: How do you know whether someone is better off when they choose to consume a product that has negative effects on them? This is especially germane to tobacco and e-cigarettes, but it's also relevant for a wide range of consumer goods and services, ranging from soda to social media to video games. Some people (including many economists) would say that anyone who chooses to consume a product must gain utility from it, because after all they chose to consume it. Others would say that when people become addicted to something like tobacco that causes disease and early death, they are worse off as a result. In our Juul example, we took this latter approach.

Once you've decided whether something is actually beneficial or harmful for people, how do you measure utility? How do you compare it across people? How do you know what the shape of the utility function is (i.e., how do you measure marginal utility)? And, perhaps most importantly, how do you predict the consequences of your decision for a broad set of stakeholders throughout society?

All of these are important issues for applied consequentialist reasoning, because the way we measure utilities can tip the scales in favor of one alternative over another. Making matters worse, the way people estimate consequences can be distorted by various psychological factors we discussed in Chapters 2–4. For instance, we might overweight the consequences our actions have on members of our ingroup. Or, we might conduct a consequentialist analysis in a self-serving way to rationalize whatever decision we feel like making. As we will discuss in the next chapter, one way to obviate these thorny problems of measurement is to construct values-based principles that stand on their own rather than being based on consequences.

Another drawback of consequentialist reasoning is that it is not immediately sensitive to *distribution* and *rights*. If you care primarily about consequences (i.e., ends), then you can easily slip into concluding that the ends justify the means.

Consequentialism is all about maximizing the aggregate well-being of people in society. This is not the same as maximizing the wealth or GDP of a society – as we noted earlier, an extra $1,000 means much more to a poor person than to a millionaire. So consequentialists care about the distribution of wealth in society, not just the total amount of wealth. That said, they still would be willing to reduce the well-being of some people who are already badly off, if doing so would have a large positive effect on the happiness of others who are already doing fine. Yet, a values-based leader might object to that approach.

A related issue is that consequentialism does not hold that people have inalienable rights. To utilitarians, rights are only valuable if they have positive overall consequences for society. For example, John Stuart Mill argued that individual freedoms of thought, speech, and personal conduct are essential for promoting happiness and human flourishing.[6] This notion that rights are instrumental rather than innate clashes strongly with many of our moral intuitions, because there are many situations where we would be uncomfortable violating someone's rights even if the overall consequences were positive.

You might have heard about the "trolley problem," a moral dilemma made famous by the philosophers Philippa Foot and Judith Jarvis Thomson.[7] In the trolley problem, a decision maker has to choose between letting a trolley kill five people, or flipping a switch that diverts the trolley onto a different track, so that it only kills one person. When asked what they would do, many people report that they would be comfortable flipping the switch. Yet think of what such a decision implies. It does not respect the rights of the one person who is sacrificed for the greater good, and who had no say in the matter.

Consider an extreme version of the trolley problem. A healthy patient comes into the emergency room. There are five other patients who will die unless they receive organ transplants. If you were a doctor in the ER, would you be comfortable killing the healthy patient and harvesting their organs to save five lives? Probably not, even if you knew nobody would ever find out about it. Yet, this is what a consequentialist mode of reasoning may support, at least from an act utilitarian perspective. At the same time, think of the opposite edge case. Would you flip the switch if it meant saving one billion lives? Most people would say "yes" even though they would be against the organ harvesting. These tensions are what makes values-based leadership challenging.

We mention these limitations not to denigrate consequentialism. Carefully weighing consequences is an important aspect of being a values-based leader. In fact, it's hard to think of tough decisions we've made where we haven't considered consequences. Yet, hopefully this chapter has shown that it may not be appropriate to *only* consider consequences. In the next two chapters, we will present alternative ways of thinking about values. Seeing a range of different frameworks will expand your toolkit as you develop and articulate a personalized values system that is meaningful to you.

CODA

Most crucially, when you find yourself or others in your company talking like a consequentialist, be sure to be analytically rigorous. Take into account factors such as long term vs. short term consequences, marginal utilities, and multiple stakeholders and alternatives. It's very easy to declare that we're "making the world a better place." But if you care about your company's impact in the world, it's important to assess that impact carefully and systematically.

TAKEAWAYS

1. One way of leading with your values is to weigh the consequences of your actions. To avoid being subject to various psychological biases, it's important to evaluate consequences in a rigorous and analytical manner.

2. A key aspect of consequentialist analysis is to list a wide range of alternatives to the status quo as well as stakeholders that can be affected by our actions. Although there are practical constraints to the number of alternatives and stakeholders to consider, people often err by limiting their thinking rather than expanding it. A values-based leader thinks broadly about alternatives and stakeholders.

3. After identifying affected stakeholders, alternatives can be evaluated relative to the status quo by estimating the net benefits to each group of stakeholders, and then summing the net benefits. If the overall net benefits are positive, then the alternative is preferred to the status quo.

4. In calculating net benefits, we should consider the philosophical and economic principle of utility, or well-being. In evaluating net benefits, it is important to consider both long-term as well as short-term consequences, in addition to assessing marginal utilities.

5. There are limitations to consequentialist thinking, particularly if we do not believe that the ends justify the means. Consequentialism is not immediately sensitive to distribution and rights, two things we should consider as values-based leaders.

SUGGESTIONS FOR FURTHER READING

A classic, and highly readable, statement of consequentialist philosophy is John Stuart Mill's *Utilitarianism*. The most influential contemporary consequentialist is Peter Singer, who has written a variety of highly provocative pieces, such as *Animal Liberation: A New Ethics for Our Treatment of Animals* as well as "The Singer Solution to World Poverty."

His book *Practical Ethics* applies consequentialist reasoning to a wide range of contemporary ethical issues. An interesting take on consequentialism is *Moral Tribes: Emotion, Reason, and the Gap between Us and Them*, by Joshua Greene, who argues that utilitarianism is the fundamental unifying principle across ethical systems.

REFLECTIVE EXERCISES

1. Think of a controversial decision made by the leaders of your company, organization, or university. Analyze this decision through the lens of consequentialism, using the framework from this chapter. First, be specific about the status quo and at least one possible alternative course of action. Second, list the affected stakeholders. Third, assess the effects on each group of stakeholders. Finally, sum up the net benefits and costs, and make a recommendation for what the decision makers should do. Also, think about how to explain your recommendation to decision makers, in a way that they would find compelling.

2. If your own personal values include making the world a better place, think about how your career trajectory aligns with your values. Is it important to you to have a job that actively promotes your values? If your company aligns with your values, how do you articulate those values in your role as a leader? Alternatively, do you view making an impact as something you do outside your professional life, for example by volunteering or donating to charity?

7

Perspective-Taking

Opioids are a powerful tool for relieving pain and preventing suffering. But they also can cause addiction, and in the early 2000s the United States experienced a massive opioid epidemic, leading to over 400,000 deaths.[1] For many of the millions who survived addiction, the experience was miserable. Medical bioethicist Travis Reider, who became addicted while undergoing a series of surgeries after his foot was crushed in a motorcycle accident, said that as he went through withdrawal "every moment in those four weeks was the worst moment of my life." It was so bad that for his final surgery he decided to suffer through excruciating post-operation pain rather than take opioids to treat it.[2]

Opioid manufacturers and distributors – most famously Purdue Pharma, but also many others including McKesson, Johnson & Johnson, CVS, Walgreens, and Walmart – have come under intense scrutiny for their role in the epidemic. Manufacturers have been criticized for misleading marketing, as well as kickback schemes for doctors. Major distributors failed to address localized spikes in prescriptions that were being funneled to the black market, including some "pill mill" pharmacies in rural areas that supplied hundreds of pills per resident each year.

A consequentialist analysis, as described in Chapter 6, would weigh the positive and negative effects of opioids and say that manufacturers and distributors have a responsibility to carefully analyze how they market the drugs and to track patterns of prescriptions, with the goal of minimizing the harms of opioids while still providing pain relief for people who need it.

But consequentialist reasoning isn't the only way people assess companies' behavior. Many people find it especially disturbing that Purdue

Pharma knew their drug OxyContin was highly addictive and being used on the black market. Yet, as the company later admitted in court, Purdue continued to fraudulently market it as being "less addictive, less subject to abuse and diversion, and less likely to cause tolerance and withdrawal than other pain medications."[3]

A related concern is that companies didn't respect patients and were just using them to make money, without concern for their health and safety. California Attorney General Xavier Becerra, who was later appointed by President Joe Biden as Secretary of Health and Human Services, captured these sentiments when he announced a lawsuit against Purdue Pharma and its former President, Dr. Richard Sackler, saying: "Purdue's deliberate and deceptive marketing and sale of these drugs sacrificed the wellbeing of Californians for billions of dollars in profits and fueled an unprecedented national public health crisis."[4] Note that these concerns are not just about the *consequences* of opioids, but also about the *motives* of manufacturers and distributors.

The idea that motives matter is quite intuitive. But once we move past easy cases (e.g., whether it's morally acceptable to intentionally deceive people about the risks of opioid addiction), we need a structure to think systematically about motives and assess their legitimacy. What does it mean to have good motives? After all, everyone probably thinks *their* motives are good, given the need to preserve a positive self-image (see Chapter 3). So how do we know whether our own motives are legitimate? And what does it mean to treat people well? These are key questions for values-based leaders, and they are the questions we will address in this chapter.

Perhaps the most famous statement of our responsibilities to others is the Golden Rule, the idea that we should treat others the way we want to be treated. Although the phrase "the golden rule" originated in Christian theology, the idea is present in the teachings and sacred texts of many religions, some of which are probably familiar to you:

- "Hurt not others in ways that you yourself would find hurtful." *Udana-Varga* 5:18 (Buddhism).
- "Do to others what you would have them do to you." *Matthew* 7:12 (Christianity).
- "What you do not want done to yourself, do not do to others." *Analects* 15:24 (Confucianism).
- "This is the sum of duty: do not do to others what would cause pain if done to you." *Mahabharata* 5:1517 (Hinduism).

- "None of you believes until he wishes for his brother what he wishes for himself." *An-Nawawi's Forty Hadith* 13 (Islam).
- "You shall love your neighbor as yourself." *Leviticus* 19:18 (Judaism).

Of course, there are important differences among these statements, and generations of religious scholars have debated their meaning as well as how to apply them in practice. But they share a common theme: We shouldn't just be motivated by our own interests and desires – we also must put ourselves in others' shoes and see things from their perspective.

Perspective-taking is an important general skill for effective leadership, whether we're trying to mentor an employee, resolve a dispute, design an innovative product, or inspire a team. In fact, it's a useful skill even for leaders who don't care at all about values. But, as suggested by the Golden Rule and its ubiquity across the moral thinking of many human civilizations, perspective-taking plays an especially crucial role in values-based leadership.

In this chapter, we develop ways of assessing motives systematically, grounded in perspective-taking. If you've studied philosophy, you'll recognize that our approach draws loosely on the ideas of Immanuel Kant, who objected to consequentialist reasoning and argued that it's possible to reason through whether actions are right or wrong, independent of their consequences. As in our discussion of consequentialism in Chapter 6, our goal is not to delve deeply into abstract philosophical details, but rather to provide concrete tools and ways of thinking that you can use to become a better values-based leader. We'll do this by developing two tests for taking others' perspectives into account when assessing a course of action that you're considering.

WHAT IF EVERYONE DID THIS?

In business and in our personal lives, we constantly give reasons for our actions. Sometimes, as we discussed in Chapter 3, these are mere rationalizations or attempts to concoct justifications for things we feel like doing. But sometimes a reason is actually intended to be a serious argument that our purposes or motives give our actions moral legitimacy.

If we intend such an argument to be taken seriously, and to be compelling to others, then we have to think about it from their perspective, not just our own. This has important implications. In particular, taking other people's perspective makes it pretty clear that if it's morally acceptable for me to do something then it's also morally acceptable for others to do it.

To say otherwise is to claim that I'm special and I get to act according to a different set of rules than everyone else. Although special privileges for certain individuals like kings and queens have been present in many societies throughout history, most people nowadays consider them to be morally indefensible.

This suggests the following test for whether our motives justify our behavior: *What if everyone did this? Would I still achieve the goals that motivate my action if other people behaved the way I'm behaving?* If achieving my goals is only possible when others refrain from doing what I'm doing, this suggests that whatever reasons I'm giving to justify my actions are simply an attempt to exempt myself from general rules of good behavior. The "*What if everyone did this?*" test thus serves as a powerful antidote to our natural human tendency to concoct self-serving rationalizations for our actions.

So far, the way we've described the test is fairly abstract, so let's make it concrete by applying it to specific situations. For starters, consider Purdue Pharma's marketing claim that OxyContin didn't cause addiction. Making this claim only helped the company achieve its goals – namely increasing sales and profits – because people trust claims made by pharmaceutical companies. If every company that wanted to boost its sales made false claims about the effectiveness and safety of its drugs, then nobody would believe those claims. In fact, that's exactly what happens in some countries that, unlike the United States, lack effective government oversight of the industry: Many companies make false claims about their drugs, the market is flooded with counterfeits, and a company's claims about safety and efficacy don't convince consumers to buy its products. Thus, the "*What if everyone did this?*" test concludes that Purdue's behavior was unethical.

The test also can be applied to promises and verbal contracts, in both personal and business relationships. As an example, suppose two MBA students, call them Jessie and Peyton, start dating in their last year of business school. They both get great job offers, but Jessie's job is in Jakarta and Peyton's is in Prague. The relationship seems to be going well, so they both would like to locate in the same city. Peyton comes up with a solution: Jessie will defer the job in Jakarta for a year (something the employer is OK with) to come to Prague, and Peyton promises that after a year in Prague they'll move together to Jakarta and live happily ever after. However, Peyton has no intention of ever moving to Jakarta, and assumes Jessie will end the relationship the moment this becomes clear. Along the way, though, Peyton figures it will be enjoyable to continue the romantic relationship with Jessie during school and for a few months after they move to Prague. Is it OK for Peyton to deceive Jessie about their plans to move to Jakarta?

Applying the *"What if everyone did this?"* test, the answer is no, because if everyone felt free to deceive their romantic partners about their plans and commitments, then nobody would believe promises made by people they're dating. Peyton's deception is only effective because it violates a social norm that it's wrong to deceive others in this way. In other words, lies are only effective because people generally assume that others are telling the truth.

The same sort of issue arises not just in personal relationships but in a wide range of business relationships. When hiring, is it acceptable to deceive applicants about working conditions and opportunities for advancement? When a company is seeking government approval to operate a mine or build a factory, is it OK to promise to hire local talent for key management roles and then bring in expats instead? How about hiring a contractor to work on a construction project, and then trying to get out of paying them once the work is complete? Or is it OK for a private equity firm to acquire a company from its founders, tell them it plans to keep the company on its current course, and then fire people and sell off divisions as soon as the deal is complete? And, at the most general level, is it acceptable for people to make promises and verbal agreements that they intend to renege on? According to the *"What if everyone did this?"* test, all of these behaviors are unethical.

Another behavior that violates the test is theft. Shoplifters take advantage of the fact that most people are honest and pay for goods and services. If everyone decided that it was OK to steal, then retail establishments would go out of business – and it would then be impossible to steal anything. Or, stores would invest so much in security that shoplifting would be thwarted. Note that, in contrast, an act utilitarian analysis may justify theft in some situations, such as a poor person stealing bread to feed their family.

Classic examples of theft in the business world include patent and copyright infringement, as well as wage theft. In the case of drug patents, if other companies infringed on a pharmaceutical company's intellectual property whenever they wanted without paying for it, then companies wouldn't invest in development of new drugs, and there would be no intellectual property to steal.

The *"What if everyone did this?"* test provides a way to assess these sorts of behaviors. In a wide range of circumstances, the test concludes that it's wrong to engage in outright deception and that we have a responsibility to make a good-faith effort to follow through on our promises and verbal agreements. Generally speaking, behaviors such as lying, stealing, and cheating do not pass this test.

AM I JUST USING THEM?

Another way to think about perspective-taking, in the spirit of the golden rule, is to recognize and take seriously the fact that other people have their own goals and objectives. Treating them with respect and dignity requires interacting with them in a way that treats them as ends, not just as a means for achieving our own purposes. After all, that's how we'd want to be treated if we were in their shoes.

Or, as put by Susan Fowler, who wrote a famous 2017 blog post about Uber's hostile work environment and rampant sexual harassment: "The way I like to think about it is you recognize that everybody is the protagonist in their own story. And they should be. You should never treat people as these secondary characters who are just helping you achieve your dreams. You should never treat people as just a cog in the machine. You should treat them as whole people."[5]

This suggests the following test for our interactions with other people: *Am I just using them as a means to achieve my own objectives, without any consideration for whether they too benefit from the interaction?*

Voluntary economic exchanges typically are acceptable according to the *"Am I just using them?"* test. For example, if you hire an accountant, you're treating them as a means to achieve your goal of balancing your books and calculating your taxes. But you're also treating them as an end, because they freely choose to work for you in order to achieve their own goals, namely earning money. In that way, you too serve as a means to their goals.

So, what sort of behavior is problematic according to this test? Extreme cases are human rights violations, like using the labor of people who are subject to coercion, either as political prisoners or as victims of human trafficking in industries like fishing, domestic work, hospitality, construction, and agriculture.

The *"Am I just using them?"* test also says it's wrong to make promises with the intention of reneging or to deceive people about key pieces of information that are relevant to their decisions. For example, someone who pretends to be committed to a romantic relationship but plans to end it once it's no longer convenient for them (like Peyton in our earlier example) is just using the person they're dating. The test would similarly say it's not acceptable to secretly withhold from business partners key pieces of information that are relevant to their assessment of whether a deal is in their interest.

In the opioids example from the start of the chapter, Purdue Pharma's approach to marketing OxyContin fails the *"Am I just using them?"* test. The company suppressed information about the risks of addiction because it was just using customers as a source of revenue, not thinking of them as patients who needed appropriate information to make well-informed decisions about pain management. Some executives at other companies that produced and distributed opioids showed callous indifference to the suffering caused by their products. As reported by the *Washington Post*, a vice president for sales at KeySource Medical, a major distributor, emailed "Keep'em comin! Flyin' out of here. It's like people are addicted to these things or something. Oh, wait, people are," to which an executive at Mallinckrodt, the largest manufacturer of opioids, replied "Just like Doritos keep eating. We'll make more."

DIFFERENT APPROACHES, DIFFERENT IMPLICATIONS

One thing you may wonder is whether the approaches to ethical reasoning that we have covered in this chapter and the previous one lead to the same conclusions. Sometimes they do. For example, the behavior of opioid manufacturers and distributors had bad consequences (widespread addiction and death) and it also failed our perspective-taking tests.

But sometimes different ethical frameworks lead to different conclusions. For example, consider a situation that Katy Waldman of *Slate.com* calls "The Confidante's Dilemma," a variant of which goes as follows.[6] A coworker tells you that their boss is sexually harassing them in ways that are clearly inappropriate and illegal. At the end of the conversation, they ask you not to tell HR or senior management, because they are afraid of retribution if people think they're "rocking the boat." They hate being harassed, but they fear that the negative career consequences of raising the issue would be even worse. You think their fears are well-founded, and you promise not to tell anyone.

Later, you start considering the consequences of not reporting the harassment. Your coworker trusted you to keep the secret but doing so means the harassment will go unaddressed. Given that many harassers are repeat offenders, their boss probably will continue to harass them, as well as others in the future. In contrast, if you report the harassment, their boss may be reprimanded or fired, and there's a greater chance that the company will actively work to eliminate harassment. From a consequentialist perspective, there's a pretty strong argument that you should report the harassment. In fact, this sort of reasoning underlies mandatory reporting rules, which some governments and companies have adopted to require people to report instances of harassment that they hear about.

But if you report your coworker's experiences, you would be violating their trust, pulling them involuntarily into an intrusive HR process, hurting their career, and forcing them to relive the trauma of the harassment. The end you'd be trying to achieve is surely a good one – eliminating future harassment – but you'd definitely be using them as a means to that end. If you look at things from their perspective, that wouldn't be OK.

This is a situation where well-meaning people can legitimately disagree about the right course of action, just as they can legitimately disagree about what should be done in the trolley problem that we mentioned at the end of Chapter 6. The answer you end up embracing ultimately depends on your values and the importance that you place on individuals vs. overall consequences.

LIMITATIONS OF THE TWO TESTS

The two tests that we have presented in this chapter address many of the critiques of consequentialist reasoning that we discussed in Chapter 6. In contrast to consequentialism, there is no need to aggregate and weigh a vast array of different effects that may be difficult to measure or predict. Moreover, the *"Am I just using them?"* test provides a strong and direct foundation for thinking about individual rights.

That said, each of the two tests has serious limitations. The *"What if everyone did this?"* test provides guidance on some issues, like theft, fraud, and deception, but is difficult to apply to most ethical issues that business leaders encounter. This is because the test produces a limited number of bright lines, rather than forcing leaders to think about the full set of consequences of their actions, both positive and negative. For instance, a company would violate the test if it purposefully hid information about the harmfulness and addictiveness of its products – as tobacco companies did starting in the 1960s – but would not violate the test if it transparently marketed potentially harmful products (e.g., video games, gambling, or alcohol).

The *"Am I just using them?"* test, in contrast, feels like it's more broadly applicable. However, it's less analytically rigorous, because we need to rely on our judgment about whether we're treating someone solely as a means. For example, suppose you are leading a successful company in a country where many people live in extreme poverty. Also, suppose you pay your low-level employees the prevailing market wage, which is barely enough for them to buy food to feed their families. You could say you're treating your employees as ends, not just as a means to your own profits, because the wages they earn enable them to survive. But a critic could say that anyone who is struggling to stay alive is in an inherently coercive situation, and that the choice between a job or possible starvation is not a real choice, so your company is just using its low-level employees as a means. The *"Am I just using them?"* test doesn't provide any guidance on how to resolve this debate. In contrast, the consequentialist approach from Chapter 6 provides a very straightforward answer: Your company should forego some profits and pay higher wages to the low-level employees, because even a small increase in pay would dramatically improve their well-being.

This leads us to another limitation of the two tests in this chapter: The fact that they don't consider consequences. Pretty much everyone cares about consequences, at least to some degree. Maybe when thinking about the trolley problem you wouldn't be willing to sacrifice one life to save five. But what if flipping the switch would save five thousand people? Or five million? At some point you'd probably think the morally right thing to do is to sacrifice one individual for the greater good. This is a contrived scenario, but the relevance of consequences isn't just a matter of abstract philosophy and hypotheticals. When we teach, we see that our students find it almost impossible to ignore consequences when discussing the right thing to do in different business situations.

A final, and very different, limitation of the two tests is that they are characterized by *omission bias*. They emphasize not doing wrong: not deceiving people, not stealing from them, not mistreating them, and not violating their rights. But the requirement to do no wrong leaves open a wide range of different courses of action. Among those paths, it doesn't provide any guidance about the appropriate one to take. Of course, values-based leaders want to avoid wrongdoing, but they also want to go beyond this minimal standard and actively do right. Indeed, one of the things that gives our lives and careers purpose is that we actively make a positive impact on the world.

APPLICATION: COLLEGE FOOTBALL

Having discussed two perspective-taking tests as an alternative to conse-quentialism, we'll now apply these ethical frameworks to a massive and highly profitable industry. US college football is big business, with billions of dollars of annual revenue from ticket sales, apparel licensing, and television deals. The money is spent on many things, including stadiums, training facilities, and travel. A lot of money ($1.1 billion in 2017) goes to scholarships and living expenses for athletes, not just in football but also in other men's and women's sports that are cross-subsidized by football revenue. An even greater amount ($1.4 billion) goes to salaries for coaches in various sports, with head football coaches in top-tier programs typically earning salaries between $4 million and $10 million.[7] In many states, the football coach of the flagship public university is the highest-paid public employee.

College football has been criticized on a variety of fronts. At some schools, players are pushed to focus on the sport so intensely that they don't get a solid education and run the risk of failing to complete their college degrees. Some coaches deceive recruits about their chances of playing and the nature of the education they'll receive. The players are also at substantial risk of concussions and chronic traumatic encephal-opathy (CTE), a devastating degenerative brain condition.

The business model for college football has also come under scrutiny, because although the players generate enormous amounts of revenue, only a small portion of it goes the players themselves. They get scholar-ships, food, and housing, but universities are accused of using the pretense of the "student athlete" to collude with each other and make money off the players' labor, without having to pay them anything close to their market value. (As a point of contrast, around half of all revenue in professional football goes to player salaries.)

A consequentialist analysis suggests there are things that could be done better in college football, like improving safety, earnings, and educational outcomes for players. But overall, despite its flaws, the sport actually looks pretty good, because most players love playing football and the games give great joy to millions of fans.

In contrast, the perspective-taking tests that we developed in this chapter paint the sport in a much more negative light. In particular, there's a pretty strong case to be made that the treatment of college football players fails the *"Am I using them?"* test, and that universities just see them as a means to achieve championships, glory, and revenue.

From the perspective of some players, this is definitely the case. In August 2020, a group of players from schools in the Pac-12 Conference, including Stanford, published a letter threatening to opt out of playing the fall season. They objected to the economic structure of college athletics, the exploitation of athletes, the disproportionate impact on Black athletes, and inadequate health coverage and safety standards. At a fundamental level, their critique was that the NCAA and Pac-12 schools, which are supposed to be mission-driven educational institutions, were using them as a means, not treating them as an end. As put by Jevon Holland, a safety at the University of Oregon, "We're not your entertainment, we're human beings."[8]

The COVID-19 pandemic put things in especially sharp relief. Many football players wanted to continue to play, but others expressed concerns about whether schools really had their interests at heart. After coming under intense pressure, some conferences, including the Pac-12, announced that they were postponing or canceling the season, with commissioner Larry Scott saying "We have a responsibility to protect our players, and given what we still don't know about the spread of the virus, we simply couldn't play football and look parents in the eye and say, 'We've got your kids' best interests in mind.'"[9] But other conferences, including powerhouses like the Big-12 and SEC, brought their football players on campus, held physically intense workouts, and prepared to play a full season of games.

In a scathing *Sports Illustrated* article, Rohan Nadkarni wrote: "In some cases, schools are asking students to stay at home and take classes online while still asking athletes to play football games. Other schools are asking players to sign waivers absolving them of any liability involving COVID-19. The universities are making decisions without formalized input from players – unlike the return of every other sport – because the conference commissioners, athletic directors and coaches have too much money on the line not to play."

As classes started in September 2020, it became clear that colleges were a major breeding ground for COVID-19, and several football teams experienced outbreaks. Nonetheless, once the football season got underway in late September, the Pac-12 and all other major conferences that had postponed their seasons changed their minds and decided that they would play games after all.

CODA

Perspective-taking is a generally useful habit for effective leadership in a wide range of organizational settings. Leaders who value the rights and well-being of individuals engage in perspective-taking not only for strategic purposes, but also to assess whether they are living up to their values. When done well, this can help us overcome our tendency to generate self-serving rationalizations for our actions and ensure that we treat people with respect and dignity.

TAKEAWAYS

1. One way of leading with your values is to assess the motives that underlie your actions. Seeing things from others' perspectives is important for assessing the legitimacy of the reasons behind your actions.

2. A test that can be used to assess an action, taking others' perspectives into account, is *"What if others did this?"* If an action is acceptable for you, it's also acceptable for others. And if achieving your goals requires that other people don't act the way you do, then maybe there's something problematic about your motives.

3. Another test that can be used to assess your motives when interacting with others is *"Am I just using them?"* This test recognizes the importance of treating other people as ends, not solely as means.

4. The results of these tests don't always align with consequentialist reasoning. When the different modes of reasoning diverge, well-meaning values-based leaders can have legitimate, principled differences of opinion about the right course of action.

5. The perspective-taking tests have limitations, partly because they don't consider consequences. Also, although they rule out some actions as unethical, they don't provide guidance about how to do right as opposed to just avoiding doing wrong.

SUGGESTIONS FOR FURTHER READING

Even by the standards of academic philosophy, Immanuel Kant's treatises are difficult reading. A reasonably accessible introduction is "Kant's Moral Philosophy" from the online *Stanford Encyclopedia of Philosophy*, https://plato.stanford.edu/entries/kant-moral/. At a more applied level, and in a context (sexual harassment) that is far too common in the business world, Katy Waldman's *Slate.com* article "The Confidante's Dilemma" draws a clear contrast between consequentialism and concerns over using people as a means. In popular culture, the TV show *The Good Place* features many scenarios that draw on consequentialism, Kant's notions of duty, as well as other normative ethical philosophies.

REFLECTIVE EXERCISES

1. Think of a situation where someone deceived you. Was it ethical of them to deceive you? Why or why not?
2. Think of a situation where you deceived someone. Was it ethical of you to deceive them? Why or why not?
3. If you gave different answers to questions 1 and 2, was there anything fundamentally different about the two situations?
4. If you are a devoutly religious person, how do you interpret your religion's teachings about how to treat others? What guidance do they give you about your responsibilities to others?
5. What would you do in the "confidante's dilemma"? If you have experienced this dilemma in the past, how did you approach it? Looking back, do you feel that you did the right thing? And what could you do better in the future?

8

Being Fair

People often demand that leaders be "fair." But what exactly does fairness mean? What Person A perceives as fair often strikes Person B as unfair, particularly if Person A is the "winner" and Person B is the "loser" in a situation. One of the biggest challenges that leaders face in organizations is the clarion call of "But that's not fair!" In this chapter, we will delve into the concept of fairness, motivated by philosophical theories of justice.

A company's policies, rules, and institutions have tremendous effects on how benefits and burdens are distributed across its stakeholders, including employees, customers, shareholders, and members of society at large. When setting internal company policies that affect different sets of employees, leaders need to be keenly attuned to concepts of justice and fairness. At the same time, corporations exist within the broader context of society (see Chapter 5). Thus, issues of fairness also emerge when thinking about the role of the firm in society, including how the firm influences government policies and affects social justice.

Many firm-level decisions come down to the issue of distribution: Given that resources are scarce, who gets what and why? The consequentialist framework for values-based leadership that we covered in Chapter 6 focused on increasing the total well-being of people in society. However, in Chapter 7, we noted that leading with your values also means considering whether people's rights and autonomy are violated. In this chapter, we will attempt to balance these considerations. In addition to increasing overall human happiness, fairness requires that we think about the distribution of happiness among people and the procedures we use that determine who gets what.

Recall from Chapter 2 that fairness is one of the core moral intuitions of human beings. But when people use the word "fairness," they often mean very different things. The moral psychologist Jonathan Haidt offers a useful summary for how people think about fairness. Some people think about fairness as *equality of outcomes*. Others think about fairness in terms of equality of opportunity, or *procedural fairness*.[1] Does everyone have the same opportunity given their talents and motivation, even if people's outcomes end up being highly unequal? As we will discuss later, this tension between equality of outcomes and equality of opportunity is at the heart of many debates around fairness in organizations, including both for-profit businesses as well as nonprofits. Some people believe that equality of opportunity is an empty promise unless it is accompanied by other policies that help level the playing field and reduce inequality in outcomes. Others believe that even in the presence of procedural fairness major inequalities are an inherent aspect of modern market-based economies.

People also think about fairness in a third way – *fairness as proportionality*. In other words, do people get what they deserve? People who subscribe to this view of fairness believe that hard workers should be rewarded and slackers should be punished. Proportionality is central to the debate over a thorny word: equity. If you look up "equity" in the *Merriam-Webster* dictionary, you get a very unhelpful definition: "fairness or justice in the way people are treated." In other words, a tautology. Some people think it is equitable to be proportional and that people should be rewarded and punished based on their actions. Others think equity requires intervening to reduce disparities in people's outcomes.

Once you clarify the amorphous term "fairness" in these three concrete ways, you can see why people often view the same policy in different ways. For instance, some people view affirmative action as crucial to ensuring both equality of outcomes and equality of opportunities whereas others see preferential hiring as violating procedural fairness and proportionality. We'll delve more deeply into these debates later in the chapter.

Closely tied to the idea of fairness are the concepts of *positive liberty* and *negative liberty*. Negative liberty is the freedom to be left alone – to be free from someone else violating your rights. On the other hand, positive liberty is having the power and resources to be able to achieve your goals. This often requires *not* leaving people alone and instead taking explicit actions to address inequalities. Similar to how people have different interpretations of what it means to be "fair," people have differing views on what it means to be "free." For some people, being free means not having other people tell you what to do or how to spend your money. For others, to truly be free, you need to have the opportunity to achieve success regardless of your identity and background, and it is not enough to simply be "left alone."

Throughout this chapter, we'll present competing frameworks of justice and apply them to real-life business situations. As you'll see, there are no easy answers. Fairness is one of the most important qualities of an effective leader – yet it is hard to universally be viewed as "fair." This is not only because people have self-serving biases, that is, they think it's unfair if they don't get what they want. People also have differing, sincere, deeply held views of the meaning of fairness and justice.

THE "OVARIAN LOTTERY"

Warren Buffett, the multi-billionaire and famed investor, often talks about the "ovarian lottery" at shareholder meetings for Berkshire Hathaway, when speaking to MBA students, and in his books. (Given the gendered nature of that phrase, a more enlightened wording would be the "zygote lottery.") In 2013, he explained the concept to an audience at the University of Maryland:

Just imagine that it is 24 hours before you are born. A genie comes and says to you in the womb, "You look like an extraordinarily responsible, intelligent, potential human being. Going to emerge in 24 hours and it is an enormous responsibility I am going to assign to you – determination of the political, economic, and social system into which you are going to emerge. You set the rules, any political system, democracy, parliamentary, anything you wish, can set the economic structure, communistic, capitalistic, set anything in motion and I guarantee you that when you emerge this world will exist for you, your children, and grandchildren.

What's the catch? One catch – just before you emerge you have to go through a huge bucket with 7 billion slips, one for each human. Dip your hand in and that is what you get – you could be born intelligent or not intelligent, born healthy or disabled, born black or white, born in the US or in Bangladesh, etc. You have no idea which slip you will get.

But not knowing which slip you are going to get, how would you design the world? Do you want men to push around females? It's a 50/50 chance you get female. If you think about the political world, you want a system that gets what people want. You want more and more output because you'll have more wealth to share around. The US is a great system, turns out $50,000 GDP per capita, 6 times the amount when I was born in just one lifetime. But not knowing what slip you get, you want a system that once it produces output, you don't want anyone to be left behind. You want to incentivize the top performers, don't want equality in results, but do want something that those who get the bad tickets still have a decent life. You also don't want fear in people's minds – fear of lack of money in old age, fear of cost of health care.

I call this the "Ovarian Lottery." My sisters didn't get the same ticket. Expectations for them were that they would marry well, or if they work, would work as a nurse, teacher, etc. If you are designing the world knowing 50/50 male or female, you don't want this type of world for women – you could get female.

Design your world this way; this should be your philosophy.[2]

While Buffett explains the concept of "the ovarian lottery" with panache and clarity, the idea is not his. He took it from the philosopher John Rawls. In 1971, Rawls published *A Theory of Justice*, one of the most important nonfiction books ever written, one that has framed public policy debates for the past half century. Rawls's theory is a political philosophy, intended to guide our understanding of how society as a whole should be organized. There are two ways to apply this concept to management. First, one can consider intra-organizational justice, treating the firm, for example, as Rawls treats society at large. Second, one can consider the firm within the social environment and take into account companies' interactions with broader groups of stakeholders.

Rawls's central claim is that for a policy to be just it should be designed from behind an imaginary *veil of ignorance*. The veil of ignorance is a sort of thought experiment. Imagine that members of an organization met together to decide on the rules that would govern them, but that these individuals did not know what positions in the organization they would occupy. They could be the CEO, a middle manager, an entry-level professional, or a janitor. Rawls refers to this state of ignorance as the *original position*. Rawls's argument is that the policies that people would agree on from behind the veil would be just, because people would not make self-interested decisions based upon their current positions. Behind the veil of ignorance, everyone knows they're unlikely to be CEO and much more likely to be one of the many low-level employees. Thus, a CEO who used the veil of ignorance as a tool for thinking about company policies wouldn't adopt a policy that only benefits top executives. Rawls's central insight was that much of the injustice we see in the world stems from the rules being written by powerful people who benefit from those rules.

We can intuitively observe the logic of the veil of ignorance in our everyday lives. When parents want two siblings to share a candy bar, they often set the rule: "One of you cuts and the other chooses." The child who does the cutting is basically put behind the veil of ignorance and therefore is incentivized to make the split as even as possible. One major source of injustice in the world is that cutters are also choosers.

Or think about the last time you were on a plane. A classic example of a scarce resource is that in a three-person row there are six arms but only four armrests. One rule that could be selected from behind the veil of ignorance is that the person in the middle seat gets two armrests whereas those in the aisle and window will have to make do with one. On the one hand, a view of "fairness as proportionality" would see the person in the middle as deserving that uncomfortable position because they chose to buy that ticket. However, from behind the veil of ignorance, we can imagine many reasons why we find ourselves in a middle seat. Perhaps there was a death or a family emergency and we had to book a last-minute ticket. Or maybe our original flight (with an aisle seat) was cancelled and this was one of the only seats left on the second flight. Or maybe we are not wealthy enough to pay extra for an aisle or window seat. From behind the veil, a good rule would be one that makes the middle seat slightly less uncomfortable.

Rawls doesn't just consider specific rules and policies. He also analyzes general properties of institutions that would be chosen from behind the veil of ignorance. For instance, he argues that people would choose institutions that grant people liberties and equality of opportunity. The form of equality of opportunity that Rawls argues for is not just formal equality of opportunity, that is, treating people neutrally at the moment that they apply for a job, but rather *fair equality of opportunity*, by which he means that social institutions must be set up so that all people, even those from disadvantaged backgrounds, have a reasonable chance to rise to positions of wealth and status in society.

One of Rawls's more controversial claims is that from behind the veil people would prefer something he calls the *difference principle*. The difference principle holds that policies should increase the well-being of the least-advantaged people. This is also known as the *maximin principle*, since it holds that the goal is to maximize the well-being of the minimum or least well-off person. In the case of the airplane, the people in the middle seats are least well-off compared to those in aisle and window seats.

The difference principle often implies very different decisions from a pure consequentialist analysis (Chapter 6). Remember that consequentialists want to maximize overall happiness or well-being, even if some people wind up being much better off than others. In contrast, the difference principle would select a distribution that maximized the position of the least well-off person even if that meant substantial sacrifices for those who are better off, or for society at large.

It is important to note that the difference principle does not imply pure egalitarianism or communism. It allows for inequality as long as we are maximizing the well-being of the person at the bottom. In this way, the difference principle allows for doing things that are "win-win," or changes that make everyone better off without making anyone worse off. In fact, one of Rawls's most important philosophical contributions was to provide a principled justification for inequality in capitalist societies: As long as social institutions are set up to ensure that the benefits of prosperity are shared widely, inequality is acceptable precisely because it incentivizes hard work and innovation, growing the economy in ways that can lift up the least well-off people. Of course, Rawls would be concerned if inequality got so bad that it compromised equality of opportunity – which is how some social critics would characterize the contemporary United States.

Applying Rawls's theory of justice to a management example, consider a firm contemplating whether to implement a generous parental leave policy. Recently, for instance, Facebook granted new parents four months of paid leave. One could argue that this policy was intended to recruit and retain talented employees. But the policy was far more generous than those offered by many of Facebook's competitors, so it is unlikely that labor market competition was the primary motivation. Rather, company executives like Mark Zuckerberg and Sheryl Sandberg stated that this policy was the right thing to do, both to assist new parents and to promote the advancement of women in the firm. In this way, Facebook's HR policies were intended not only to promote intra-organizational justice, but also address a key issue of social justice: The gender gap in promotions and wages.

There are many ways that a generous parental leave policy could be justified in Rawls's framework: (1) equality of opportunity – parental leave enables new parents to spend time with their newborn without having to quit their job or forego career opportunities; (2) veil of ignorance – if you imagined that you could be any person in the organization (including a young parent), you would probably support this policy; (3) difference principle – though the policy may seem to reinforce inequalities (with senior executives being paid more for staying home and being with their child than employees at the bottom of the ladder), it would still be fair because low-level employees are better off than if the policy weren't in place. An assumption here is that due to stresses in their lives, low-level employees with children are less advantaged than low-level employees without children, who may prefer bonuses rather than parental leave policies.

Although compelling, Rawls's theory is not without its critics. First, it is unclear whether the difference principle would be chosen from behind the veil of ignorance. For instance, a consequentialist may argue that people would choose to maximize aggregate happiness. The difference principle assumes that people exhibit an extremely high degree of risk aversion, preferring the maximin outcome because of the risk that they could be in the least-advantaged position. This assumption is arguably reasonable, especially since in the original position people do not know what skills and traits they would be endowed with (e.g., intelligence, grit), and these skills might be correlated with risk-seeking. Also, even setting aside questions about risk aversion, it's important to keep in mind that the least advantaged are a huge group of people. In a wealthy country like the United States, tens of millions of people live in poverty, and globally there are billions of people at the base of the economic pyramid. (The World Bank recently estimated that a quarter of the people in the world live on less than $3.20 per day and almost half live on less than $5.50 per day.)[3] So, in the ovarian/zygote lottery it's pretty likely you'd be born into poverty, and from behind the veil of ignorance it seems like a good idea to design social institutions that account for that possibility.

A second criticism is that the thought experiment of the veil of ignorance is fruitless because people likely are unable to authentically place themselves in the original position. They have lived their whole lives with particular characteristics – race, gender, socioeconomic status, and cultural background. These characteristics shape our life experiences, which in turn may influence what people think they would choose from behind the veil.[4] While this is an accurate description of human psychology, the Rawlsian fiction of the veil of ignorance is a salutary invitation to empathy and perspective-taking, which is a step in the right direction even if we cannot completely shed the biases we have due to our current position in society.

Despite these criticisms, Rawls offers a compelling methodology for thinking about what makes a just outcome. Even if one does not agree with the difference principle, one can still apply the logic of the veil of ignorance to make fair decisions as a manager. And that may well mean focusing on the least advantaged individuals, who are easy to ignore when designing both company and social policies.

FAIRNESS AS PROCESS

If we follow Rawls, we think of fairness in terms of *outcomes*. As we noted above, this isn't the only way to think of fairness. Others think of justice in terms of *process*, asking whether fair procedures are being used. And one way we can judge the fairness of a process is whether it violates people's rights and autonomy (see Chapter 7).

The most famous counterpoint to Rawls's theory of justice is Robert Nozick's process-based interpretation of fairness. In 1974, Nozick responded to Rawls in his book *Anarchy, State, and Utopia*, which is also one of the most important nonfiction books of the twentieth century. Nozick defines a just process as one based on consent and autonomy. If people make autonomous decisions that are not coerced, then any distribution of outcomes is by definition just, even if there ends up being a lot of inequality. In fact, Nozick would argue that meeting the difference principle often requires unjust actions because achieving a more equal distribution requires infringing on some people's liberties.

Nozick's famous example to explain his theory concerns the basketball player Wilt Chamberlain. To make the thought experiment more timely, consider instead LeBron James, the best basketball player of the 2010s. James freely consented to play basketball in front of millions of fans. These fans freely consented to pay their hard-earned money to watch him play. Everyone benefitted from this exchange. After these transactions took place, James ended up much wealthier than most of the fans. But was that outcome unjust even if it was unequal? Nozick would argue that the outcome was just because the process consisted of autonomous choices. In Nozick's framework, heavily taxing James and distributing that money to the fans would be considered an unjust infringement on James's liberty.

Returning to the previous example of generous paid parental leave, Nozick would argue that the company is under no ethical obligation to implement such a policy. People who have young children have the right to decide whether to work for the company and are free to leave if its parental leave policies are not conducive to their career advancement. The company could choose to adopt such policies if doing so would be useful when competing in the labor market for top-level talent, but according to Nozick the company has no ethical obligation to adopt the policies.

Nozick is of course aware that his theory, which is based on autonomy and free exchange, requires a certain starting time period. And the allocation of skills and wealth at that time period could be the result of past injustices. For example, even though the contemporary United States is largely (but not completely) characterized by free exchange, for many years, racial minority groups were restricted from owning property and building wealth. The legacy of these injustices means that Americans who are members of minority groups find it more difficult than white Americans to succeed economically.

Nozick's solution to this is *rectification*, that is, to compensate for past injustices via redistribution, and then employ a just process for exchange going forward. A major criticism of Nozick's theory is that there has never been a serious attempt at rectification that would be sufficient to make up for past injustices. Therefore, even if there are free and autonomous exchanges after a given time period, they by definition cannot be just if there were unjust violations of autonomy (e.g., slavery and discrimination) in the past. Given the history of oppression in the world, it is unlikely one could find any time period that consists of a fair initial allocation.

APPLICATION: HIRING POLICIES TO BOOST DIVERSITY

Recently, there has been immense pressure on organizations to increase the representativeness of their workforces, particularly on dimensions such as race and gender. Industries like technology and financial services, which have been sources of tremendous wealth creation, have come under particular scrutiny. Leaders at some companies have responded with initiatives to increase diversity through affirmative action in hiring.

Are these policies fair? How should they be constructed to ensure fairness? These are important questions, as leaders need to justify their hiring practices to their current employees, to the labor market, to investors, and to society at large. Before delving into the issue of fairness, let's consider what the frameworks of consequentialism and perspective-taking from Chapters 6 and 7 have to say about the issue of diversity in hiring.

Consequentialism

A consequentialist analysis of diversity initiatives would consider a wide range of effects on people who get jobs, those who don't get jobs, and long-run impacts on society as a whole. Setting aside these broader concerns, a more narrow consequentialist argument that many people make in favor of diversity hiring is that it makes a company more successful and profitable.

This is probably the most popular justification that people give for using race and gender as criteria for hiring, and business leaders often say that diversity will improve their companies' performance. Some of these claims are based on research in the social sciences. For example, Scott Page, a scholar of management, has described the returns from diversity as a "bonus." He argues that in a complex world, the best way to generate innovative solutions is not to try to choose the "best" individuals, because even if those people can be selected using unbiased meritocratic criteria they will tend to have the same approach to problem-solving. Rather, he argues, it's better to assemble a heterogeneous team comprised of people with unique perspectives. This sort of argument is often referred to as the "business case for diversity."

Let's dig a bit deeper and evaluate whether it's appropriate to make a business case for diversity. Some might view that approach as distasteful because it treats workers from underrepresented groups as simply a means to an end. That is, the policies may send a message that companies build a diverse workforce not because it's the right thing to do for society but rather for the benefit of shareholders. There are also other implications of these types of consequentialist arguments for diversity that many proponents have not fully thought through. For instance, if you were to obtain data that showed that diversity was harming organizational performance, does that mean your firm should actively try to homogenize its workforce? If diversity programs primarily rest on a business case, then the answer would be yes.

Indeed, there have long been concerns that diversity leads to conflicts and reduces social cohesion. The famous political scientist Robert Putnam found that diverse communities in the United States score lowest on metrics of civic well-being.[5] And arguments against the integration of the US armed forces – on race, gender, and sexual orientation – often relied on arguments that diversity harmed organizational performance.

Further, while people often use the "diversity is good for business" argument to advocate for targeted hiring – in favor of women and under-represented minorities – that argument actually suggests a much more holistic view of diversity. Teams presumably should be constructed to not only be diverse with respect to race and gender, but also life experience, political ideology, personality, and thinking style, among many other characteristics. But this broad view of diversity is not what many supporters of affirmative action have in mind.

Given these issues, why is the "business case for diversity" argument so popular? Most likely, the reason is strategic. It sounds good, the sort of argument that can be used to build support among a broad group of stakeholders. Current employees and managers from groups that are well represented in an organization may also support diversity out of self-interest if they believe it helps the organization as a whole. As we've discussed throughout this book, people are always trying to convince themselves that a reform is a "win-win" so that they don't have to confront difficult trade-offs.

Perspective-Taking

In terms of perspective-taking, an important goal in designing hiring policies would be to ensure that there are no conscious or unconscious biases in the hiring process, because if you put yourself in the position of a job applicant you wouldn't want to be subject to bias. In terms of specific policies, this might mean that recruiters should be blinded to applicants' personal and demographic characteristics, rather than affirmatively considering race and gender in a holistic hiring process.

Again, this is not what many proponents of diversity policies have in mind, as blind screening is not guaranteed to improve diversity. In fact, because it is blind to consequences and outcomes, it could have the effect of homogenizing the workforce with respect to race or gender. For example, although blind auditions led to a dramatic increase in the number of female musicians in symphony orchestras, they continue to have almost no Black members.

Yet, as with the consequentialist logic, the perspective-taking approach has broad appeal. After all, who wouldn't want to root out bias?

Justice

Although current discourse on the business case for diversity doesn't focus on social justice, arguments in favor of affirmative action were traditionally grounded in justice-based concerns – making up for past wrongs as well as ongoing discrimination.

Based on the arguments of Buffett and Rawls, one could construct affirmative action policies that focus on a limited set of demographic characteristics such as race and gender. From behind the veil of ignorance, we do not know what race and gender we would be assigned, so it might make sense to choose policies that favor women and underrepresented minorities, groups that are disadvantaged as a result of a long history of discrimination.

From Nozick's perspective, in contrast, a firm has no obligation to diversify its workforce, except possibly as a form of rectification for past injustices. As with the case of parental leave, a firm can choose to implement certain hiring policies if it believes that will increase its profits, but it doesn't need to be concerned with issues of fairness and social justice.

Takeaway

People have strong feelings on the issue of diversity in hiring. As we argued in Chapter 2, we think a good starting point for discussions on this issue is not to assume that people you agree with are good and people you disagree with are bad. Rather, it's better to assume that they have different, sincerely held conceptions of what is fair. Their views may of course be affected by their individual experiences, but they are also ultimately grounded in strong notions of fairness.

To some people, it is unfair if a company prioritizes hiring women and underrepresented minority group members rather than people from groups that currently dominate high pay, high status jobs. They place utmost importance on neutral equality of opportunity. There may be underrepresentation of certain groups, but the important thing is that everyone has an equal chance at a job based solely on their merit and qualifications. Some people who take this view also see affirmative action as a violation of proportionality, because they think it interferes with people getting what they deserve.

To others, this is the wrong way of looking at the issue. Instead, they see fair equality of opportunity and equality of outcomes as inexorably linked. In their view, the way to gauge whether people have equal opportunities is to see whether the outcomes are equal. If they are not, and especially if they are massively unequal, this must be due to some combination of systemic discrimination at the societal level and bias and unfairness in the particular company's hiring process. And to people who hold this view, proportionality is an unfair yardstick if the playing field is highly inequitable to begin with.

These are tough questions, and organizational leaders have been put in difficult spots on this issue, because any decision they make will strike some people as being deeply unfair. Hopefully, this discussion has helped clarify the issue and identify the key points of disagreement. At the end of the day, in your role as a leader, you need to determine which policies are consistent with your core values, and how you can authentically communicate those values – and resultant policies – to stakeholders.

In our view, a major problem is that if people don't have a good sense of their core values, then they cannot articulate coherent reasons for adopting a policy. If someone is not a consequentialist, then why are they giving consequentialist justifications? If someone claims to be outcome-blind, then why are they adopting a policy that explicitly looks at outcomes? If someone believes that policies are appropriate because that's what social justice requires, then why not just come out and say it?

On issues of diversity in hiring, as on many other issues, people are pretty adept at spotting inconsistent and inauthentic arguments made by their leaders. To be an effective leader requires having a solid understanding of values and then conveying them clearly, with both your words and your actions.

CODA

Being a leader is hard because people want to be treated "fairly" and expect leaders to construct and implement fair policies. However, everyone has different definitions of what it means for something to be "fair." Some of these are based on self-serving and ingroup biases (what helps me or my group is "fair" and any outcome where I come out with the short end of the stick is "unfair"). But people often have principled disagreements over the meaning of fairness. Navigating these disagreements is a crucial aspect of organizational leadership.

TAKEAWAYS

1. Leaders are expected to be fair, but people have different views of fairness: Fairness as equality of outcomes, procedural fairness, and fairness as proportionality. These differing views of fairness have implications for distribution – how scarce resources are divided among people.
2. Leaders are expected to construct fair policies, not only within their company but also for how their company interacts with society at large. One framework for thinking about the design of fair policies is Rawls's veil of ignorance. What policies would we select if we did not know who we were going to be in an organization or in society? Rawls argued that we would select policies that maximize the position of the least well-off individuals.
3. A competing view of fairness is justice as process. Nozick views a fair process as one that respects individual choice and autonomy. As long as no one's rights or autonomy are violated, a process is fair regardless of whether it produces unequal outcomes.

4. There are many important decisions made by organizational leaders where different theories of justice yield very different answers. Two examples are parental leave policies and policies aimed at boosting the racial and gender diversity of workforces. Many disagreements over these policies stem from competing interpretations of what it means for something to be "fair."

SUGGESTIONS FOR FURTHER READING

John Rawls's *A Theory of Justice* and Robert Nozick's *Anarchy, State, and Utopia* are modern classics on justice, fairness, public policy, and the role of the government. On the topic of diversity in hiring, the "business case for diversity" argument is nicely laid out by Scott Page in *The Diversity Bonus: How Great Teams Pay Off in the Knowledge Economy*. A great contrasting argument is the *Harvard Business Review* article "Toward a Racially Just Workplace," by Laura Morgan Roberts and Anthony J. Mayo. And for a cogent argument against hiring policies that narrowly focus on race and gender, see Zaid Jilani's article "The 'Diversity' Trap" published in *Tablet*.[6]

REFLECTIVE EXERCISES

1. What notion of justice do you find more personally compelling, Rawls's or Nozick's? Why?
2. Consider a recent disagreement about fairness that has come up in your company. What notion of fairness did people on each side of the issue rely on? Did they focus on outcomes, opportunity, proportionality, or some other criterion? Did the company's leaders make a decision that was clearly grounded in some concept of fairness? And how did they explain their decision to the employees?
3. If you work at a company that has a policy for diversity in hiring, what values form the foundation for that policy? Are the values clear? Are the company's practices well grounded in those values? If not, how should the company clarify its values or improve its practices?

9

What Are Your Core Values?

When we teach MBAs, we give them an exercise for the final day of class: We ask them to write a statement of their core values – those that will guide them in their personal lives and as leaders of organizations. We also have them read each other's statements and provide feedback. This exposes them to the diversity of values systems (even among MBAs!) and helps them get a sense of how others will react to their values. We've included this exercise at the end of this final chapter.

First, though, we want to integrate the major themes that we've covered. In the first half of the book, we examined the psychology of ethical and unethical decision-making, focusing on moral intuitions, self-serving biases, and situational pressures. Then in the second half, we focused on normative ethics, drawing on philosophical frameworks to address issues of consequences, motives, and fairness. The power of the normative frameworks does not stem solely from the analytical sharpness of the philosophers who developed them. Rather, they are powerful because they are deeply connected to human experiences and moral intuitions. Consequentialist reasoning is grounded in our concern about causing harm to others. The "*What if everyone did this?*" and "*Am I just using them?*" tests are grounded in perspective-taking and the Golden Rule. Rawls's concept of justice is grounded in a sense of fairness and Nozick's is grounded in intuitions about liberty. These connections make the normative frameworks something we can aspire to live by.

But aspiration isn't the same as execution. And it's crucial to note that there's a huge tension between normative and descriptive ethics. A major underlying theme of normative ethics is that it's not acceptable to treat oneself as special. In consequentialism, the well-being of others counts along with our own happiness. The motives tests use perspective-taking as an antidote to special treatment. Rawls's approach to justice is anchored on the idea that we could have been born in the shoes of others, including those less fortunate than ourselves. And Nozick's approach to justice requires us to respect others' autonomy.

In contrast to these normative approaches, the psychological research that we highlighted in Chapters 2–4 lays out a host of ways that we, as humans, tend to think and act as if we're special. We prioritize our own moral intuitions rather than those of others. We perceive the world in self-serving ways, think we're better than others, and overestimate the degree to which our actions and values have social support. We also seriously underestimate the degree to which situational factors can induce us to do things that are out of step with our values. All of these psychological factors make it challenging to live up to our values.

There is an additional challenge in staying true to our values in practice. The frameworks of values-based leadership that we presented in Chapters 6–8 all represent positive things that leaders should care about. Good leaders weigh the consequences of their actions. They take into account the perspective of others. And they try to be fair. The challenge arises when these values come into conflict. What should you do if a course of action produces good overall consequences but requires some deception? And would you sacrifice the overall well-being of your organization in order to treat someone fairly? There is a great temptation to assume away these sorts of trade-offs and convince ourselves that every situation is a win-win. But leaders often face tough decisions where there are winners and losers, which means that values-based actions will often be unpopular among some people. How should you resolve such decisions? We're not going to tell you what values you should have; only you can decide that. However, we strongly believe that your answers to these sorts of questions should be guided by your core values.

Part of what we have tried to do in this book is to help you think analytically about values. We hope this inspires you to reflect on – and question – your existing values systems. Then there is the challenge of figuring out what values actually mean in particular situations. Take, for example, consequences. We can all agree that we should be concerned about how our decisions affect others. But, as Chapter 6 showed, measuring, assessing, and weighing consequences is a challenging and complicated exercise. Similarly, people can abstractly talk about justice and fairness. But as explained in Chapter 8, those terms can have very different meanings to different people. By placing structure on amorphous terms such as consequences, motives, and justice, we hope to give you frameworks for applying your values in practice.

Another objective of this book is to help you anticipate and understand challenges that you will face in living up to your values. How should you go about doing that? As we suggested in Chapter 4, we don't think it helps to think about grand decisions and climactic moments in which heroes do right and villains do wrong. Most of us are neither heroes nor villains, and most of our decisions are not momentous, but rather a series of choices in our everyday lives. The key is to recognize that common-place decisions often have profound ethical content and can have a major long-run impact on whether we live according to our values.

In making day-to-day choices, we're typically surrounded by a cloud of different forces. Our values are reinforced by some of these forces, including our upbringing, our concern for others, and philosophical, literary, and religious traditions. But other forces can make it difficult to live by our values, including social pressures, stress and time pressure, misaligned incentives, poorly designed institutions and organizations, and our own self-serving biases.

The question is how to set ourselves up to be more influenced by the positive forces, so that we can live by our values. That is a highly individual question. In this book, we've laid out the fundamental challenges, but ultimately the approach you take has to be unique to your values, your experiences, your personality, and your circumstances.

Although many of the themes we have discussed are common across various philosophical, ethical, and religious traditions, this book has taken a deep dive into just a few of the world's many values systems. There are a host of different sources that you can draw from – religious texts and leaders, art, literature, movies, mentors, friends, and family. What we have done in this book is show you how to explore and evaluate values systems in a rigorous and analytical manner. In our view, thinking deeply about values is what gives them clarity. At the same time, values-based leadership is not a purely intellectual exercise. Your core values need to be authentic and meaningful to you.

DIMENSIONS OF CORE VALUES: INDIVIDUAL-LEVEL CONSIDERATIONS

Whatever values are important to you, there are various considerations to keep in mind when translating them into action.

First, what is your *objective*? Is your goal as a leader to simply avoid wrongdoing or do you seek positive impact? This ties back to the tension between consequentialism (Chapter 6) and perspective-taking (Chapter 7). Whereas consequentialist frameworks argue in favor of doing as much good as possible, motives-based frameworks are more focused on not doing wrong to specific individuals. In stating your objectives, it's important not to fall back on easy generalities like "being a good person." Rather, try to be specific, because specificity compels action.

Second, what is your *approach* to values-based leadership? Some people seek to create a set of bright-line rules that should never be broken. Our discussions of perspective-taking (Chapter 7) as well as rule utilitarianism (Chapter 6) argued in favor of certain lines in the sand regarding theft and deception. On the other hand, the downside of bright-line rules is that they do not allow leaders to exercise their discretion to tailor decisions to particular circumstances (see Chapter 6). Instead of bright lines, some leaders prefer to lay out a set of considerations they will use when making tough decisions.

Alternatively, some leaders don't even focus on decisions, but rather on a plan for personal growth so they can continually develop as a virtuous person. Someday people may write your obituary, listing your accomplishments or specific choices you made in life. But at your funeral, that's hopefully not what people will focus on. Rather, they'll talk about whether you were trustworthy, benevolent, loyal, courageous, and a good friend. These are not fixed traits; rather they are virtues that we cultivate and practice on a daily basis. But which virtues ultimately matter the most to you, personally?

Third, what is the *scope* of your considerations as a leader? Are you mainly concerned with your family and friends? Or do you care about broader groups: your company, community, country, or the world at large? Often, our self- and group-serving biases lead us to focus narrowly on ourselves and those close to us (see Chapter 3). Yet, various values-based frameworks such as consequentialism demand that we think more globally and holistically.

Fourth, how should you *tailor* your core values? Are they freestanding principles that can be easily translated and applied across time and space? Or do you need to adjust them based on cultural considerations that are unique to particular countries, regions, and industries. For instance, making facilitating payments to government officials is illegal, with strict enforcement, in many developed economies. However, in emerging markets, sometimes the unwritten rule is that facilitating payments are a necessary cost of doing business, even if there are anti-corruption laws on the books. Even if you think tailoring is necessary, be skeptical and cautious of your perceptions of cultural norms, because humans misperceive norms in systematic ways (Chapter 4).

An important aspect of tailoring is understanding your greatest fears, both about yourself and the situations you will encounter. It's easy, indeed tempting, to focus on the positive. But it's not enough to hope for the best; you also must prepare for the worst. This means reflecting honestly on the flaws and weaknesses of your character, as well as the types of situations that are most likely to bring out those weaknesses.

Another key aspect of tailoring is to think about what roles you will play in your life and career, and what approach you will take in those roles. For many people, the question of how to live a good life is fundamentally shaped by their roles as a parent, child, spouse, friend, leader, team member, or citizen.

DIMENSIONS OF CORE VALUES: ORGANIZATION-LEVEL CONSIDERATIONS

An important theme of this book is that leading with values is not just about one's personal behavior. Values-based leaders don't just do the right thing on their own. They also design organizations that steer themselves and others in the right direction. So to lead with values it's important to think about your organization's values and whether they are reflected in and reinforced by your organization's policies and culture.

As a practical matter, it's important to distinguish values-based thinking at an individual and organizational level. This is for several reasons. First, people within an organization don't necessarily have the same values, though they generally share at least some values in common. Second, people in the trenches often are skeptical of any grand pronouncements made by the higher-ups. Third, changing an organization's policies or culture is not a small task, but rather something that requires committed effort by senior leaders. Hence, it's important to think about your values at an individual level, since this will guide many personal decisions and career choices you make. At the same time, to be an effective leader of others, you cannot simply impose your values by fiat. Rather, you must balance leading with your own core values while respecting the heterogeneous viewpoints that exist within your organization.

There isn't a checklist of steps to go through as you articulate, assess, and shape an organization's values. But here are some considerations to keep in mind as you work through this complex process:

Clarify Your Company's Values. What values do you and other leaders want your company to embody? In thinking about this question, it's crucial to be realistic and honest, because your subordinates and stakeholders will quickly see through anything that sounds like it was put together by a consultant who was hired to improve the firm's image.

Assess Current Practice. Is your company actually living up to the values that you want it to embody? In particular, do the company's formal rules and informal norms encourage people to act according to the company's values? Or are things set up to drive them in a different direction – including doing things that are unethical – because that's what's expected or rewarded? And, do regular employees think that decisions made by you and other senior leaders reflect the values that you have laid out for the organization?

Answering these questions requires data. Be wary about trusting your own impressions, because even if you're an effective leader your subordinates may still sugarcoat things. To get accurate data, it's useful to do anonymous surveys to get a sense of what's being done well, what's being done badly, and what can be done better.

Align Policies with Values. If the reality of current practice in your company doesn't align with the values that you wish to establish, it's time to think about change. A useful structure for doing this is the 5 P's, which we introduced in Chapter 5. Start off by establishing Priorities, based on the values that you want your company to embody. This includes deciding what will be done when different values or interests come into conflict with each other.

Next, ask whether the other P's (Performance Metrics, Pay, Promotions, and Power) are set up to deliver on the Priorities that you set. If they're out of sync, then a crucial step is to redesign these aspects of the organization. This is likely to be a painstaking process, but without it, you can be pretty sure that the organization won't live up to the values you set.

Align Culture with Values. If your organization's culture is out of step with the values you want it to embody, how should you address this gap? Exactly how to reshape an organization's culture depends on your personal style as a leader as well as the current state of the culture and where you want it to wind up. So we can't tell you exactly how to do this.

However, we do have a few general pointers, based on key lessons from psychology.

First, be sure to communicate in ways that are authentic to your own values but also resonate with the values and moral intuitions of others in the organization. Second, don't expect perfection from others, or yourself for that matter. Your goal is not to set up an organization of heroes and angels, but rather an organization with norms and rules that encourage ordinary, fallible human beings to generally make good decisions. Third, be sure to encourage and allow dissent, rather than stamping it out. Doing so will earn the respect of your subordinates and also will give you crucial information that you need in order to continually improve the organization.

PUTTING YOURSELF IN THE RIGHT SITUATION

So far, we've talked about living by your own personal values and leading with values in an organizational context. But it's also important to keep in mind one of the most important lessons of descriptive ethics: the power of the situation (see Chapter 4). We can always hope that we'll make the heroic and unpopular decision in crunch time, regardless of the situation. But a wiser approach is to think ahead, plan, and assume that the situations we put ourselves in will have a profound effect on our behavior and our character.

Thus, one key takeaway from this book is to forge a career path that is in line with your core values. What sorts of companies, bosses, and industries align with your values? Often, when deciding what we want to do with our lives, people ask: What am I good at? And what am I passionate about? In our view, a third question is just as important: Is this job consistent with my values?

In addition to deciding what to do in our lives, we have to decide *who* to do it with. In our professional lives, this includes superiors, employees, investors, cofounders, suppliers, and clients. One criterion in deciding who to work with is whether they share your core values. Or even if they have differing values, will it be possible to fruitfully identify the sources of difference and work through them in a respectful and constructive manner, while remaining true to your own core values?

Facebook COO Sheryl Sandberg once famously told a group of Harvard MBAs: "If you're offered a seat on a rocket ship, don't ask what seat. Just get on." Her point was to put your ego aside if you have a chance to work for a truly special organization. We would make a slight addendum to Sandberg's advice. If you're offered a seat on a rocket ship, you should also be sure to ask: What kind of person is the pilot? Where are we going? And how exactly will we get there?

PARTING THOUGHTS

Values are ultimately what give meaning to our life, including the portion of it that we spend at work. It's hard to have a fulfilling career if it is not in line with your values. Similarly, it's hard to motivate and inspire employees solely with money. As disgruntled employee Peter Gibbons said in the movie *Office Space*: "My only real motivation is not to be hassled; that, and the fear of losing my job. But you know, Bob, that will only make someone work just hard enough not to get fired." People need to have a reason to follow leaders – core values are such reasons.

When people are starting out their careers, core values are often not at the top of their minds. Rather, many people worry about whether the company they are joining will grow and prosper and provide them with opportunities for advancement. These are obviously important considerations. Yet, when we talk to older alumni of the Stanford Graduate School of Business, they often wish their business school educations had been more focused on ethics and values. Purpose and meaning become increasingly salient over the course of a career, and a lifetime.

Values-based leadership is a journey, not a destination. Core values are not something you figure out once and then move forward. They evolve as we live and learn. They are shaped by experiences, successes, and hardships. What we have tried to do is equip you with psychological and philosophical knowledge. We hope this has helped you place structure on your moral intuitions, and made you attuned to the psychological factors that often compromise our good intentions. Further, we hope we have equipped you with the tools to engage and share your core values with others – not only to persuade them, but also so that you are open to persuasion yourself.

Exercise: Your Core Values and Commitments

For the final session of our MBA class, we have our students write a statement of their core values and commitments, which they share and discuss with each other. There is incredible variation in what they write. Some draw on their identity or their family history. Some draw on religious and cultural traditions. Some draw on personal or family experiences with tragedy or injustice. Some state bright-line rules for conduct, whereas others lay out general principles and priorities. Many of them find this exercise to be the most meaningful part of the class, and we agree, based on our own experiences doing the exercise ourselves.

To summarize takeaways from the chapter, here are some questions to ask yourself as you construct your statement of core values:

1. What are your goals and objectives?
2. What is your approach to values-based leadership: bright-line rules or general considerations?
3. What are the virtues that you seek to cultivate in your character?
4. What are your greatest fears, both about yourself and the situations you will encounter?
5. What roles will you play in your life and career? And what approach will you take to those roles?
6. What are your sources of guidance and inspiration?

You may want to jot down notes and let your answers to these questions percolate through your mind a bit before you proceed to the next step. Or you might want to jump in and start writing.

Writing Your Values Statement. The next step is to write a statement of your core values and the commitments that guide the decisions you make in your life and your career. When our students do this, they typically write about a page, sometimes more, sometimes less. Your statement should be personal, and meaningful to you.

As you write your values statement, you should resist the temptation to treat it as a slogan or a press release. Rather, think of it as a plan for purposeful action over the course of your career. This means it needs to be realistic and implementable. You should also take into account specific challenges that you expect to encounter.

After writing your values statement, share it with a few people close to you: family, friends, classmates, or mentors. Ask for their feedback, both about what they find compelling and meaningful, and also about the parts that strike them as unclear, contradictory, unrealistic, or impossible to implement. Use their feedback to refine and improve your statement, to make it compelling as a guide to action.

Revisiting Your Values Statement. Mark a point in your calendar to revisit your values statement and assess how well you are living up to your commitments. Each of us does this at least once a year when teaching our class. As you revisit the statement, assess how well you're doing in implementing it, and also think about how it applies to new roles you take on over the course of your life and career.

Occasionally, after major life changes or other events that make you rethink your roles and values, you may find it useful to revise your values statement. Of course, you shouldn't do this constantly – in that case, it wouldn't be a statement of commitments. But who we are isn't static, and as we grow it's good to consciously reassess our approach to living according to our values.

Notes

Chapter 1

1 Jack Nicas, "Apple Is Worth $1 Trillion; 21 Years Ago It Was on the Brink of Bankruptcy," *New York Times*, August 2, 2018, B1; Yoni Heisler, "33 Years Ago Today, Apple Launched Its IPO," *Engadget*, December 12, 2013, www.engadget.com/2013-12-12-33-years-ago-today-apple-launched-its-ipo.html.

2 Poornima Gupta and Edwin Chan, "Apple's Visionary Steve Jobs Dead at 56," *Reuters*, October 5, 2011, www.reuters.com/article/apple-jobs/wrapup-2-apples-visionary-steve-jobs-dead-at-56-idUSN1E79420Z20111006.

3 See, for example, Walter Isaacson, *Steve Jobs* (New York: Simon & Schuster, 2011).

4 Nicholas Carlson, "What It's Like to Work in China's Gadget Sweatshops Where Your iPhones and iPads Are Made," *Business Insider*, April 7, 2010, www.businessinsider.com/what-its-like-to-work-if-chinas-gadget-sweatshops-where-your-iphones-and-ipads-are-made-2010-4; Carl Levin and John McCain, "Memorandum: Offshore Profit Shifting and the U.S. Tax Code – Part 2 (Apple Inc.)", 2013, Permanent Subcommittee on Investigations, U.S. Senate; Lance Whitney, "Apple, Google, Others Settle Antipoaching Lawsuit for $415 million," *C/Net*, September 3, 2015, www.cnet.com/news/apple-google-others-settle-anti-poaching-lawsuit-for-415-million/.

5 "Apple Named 'Least Green' Tech Company," *The Guardian*, April 21, 2011, www.theguardian.com/environment/2011/apr/21/apple-least-green-tech-company; Dana Varinsky, "Apple Is the Greenest Tech Company in the World, According to Greenpeace," *Business Insider*, January 9, 2017, www.businessinsider.com/apple-greenest-tech-company-greenpeace-2017-1.

6 Yuval Noah Harari, *Sapiens: A Brief History of Humankind* (New York: Harper, 2014).

7 Max H. Bazerman and Ann E. Tenbrunsel, *Blind Spots: Why We Fail to Do What's Right and What to Do about It* (Princeton, NJ: Princeton University Press, 2011).

8 Jonathan Haidt, *The Righteous Mind: Why Good People Are Divided by Politics and Religion* (New York: Pantheon Books, 2012).

Chapter 2

1 For data on effects of immunization see: CDC, "Achievements in Public Health, 1900–1999. Impact of Vaccines Universally Recommended for Children – United States, 1990–1998," *Morbidity and Mortality Weekly Report* 48, no. 12 (1999): 243–248; CDC Center For Global Health, *2017 Annual Report*, 2017,www.cdc.gov/globalhealth/resources/reports/annual/pdf/CGH_Annual-Report_2017-h.pdf; Colette Flight, "Smallpox: Eradicating the Scourge," *BBC.com*, February 7, 2011, www.bbc.co.uk/history/british/empire_seapower/small pox_01.shtml.

2 For data on vaccination rates, see: Holly A. Hill, Laurie D. Elam-Evans, David Yankey, James A. Singleton, and Yoonjae Kang, "Vaccination Coverage among Children Aged 19–35 Months: United States, 2017," *Morbidity and Mortality Weekly Report* 67, no. 40 (2018): 1123–1128; Maggie Fox, "Vaccine Rates Are Up, but so Are Refusals," *NBCNews.com*, January 19, 2018, www .nbcnews.com/health/health-news/vaccine-rates-are-so-are-refusals-n838811.
For public opinion data see RJ Reinhart, "Fewer in U.S. Continue to See Vaccines As Important," *Gallup.com*, January 14, 2020, https://news.gallup .com/poll/276929/fewer-continue-vaccines-important.aspx.

3 Olga Khazan, "Wealthy L.A. Schools' Vaccination Rates Are As Low As South Sudan's," *The Atlantic*, September 16, 2014, www.theatlantic.com/health/arch ive/2014/09/wealthy-la-schools-vaccination-rates-are-as-low-as-south-sudans/ 380252/.

4 Lynn Harris, "Debate Intensifies over HPV Vaccine," *Salon.com*, November 24, 2005, www.salon.com/2005/11/23/hpv_vaccine_debate/.

5 The New York antivax pamphlet described in the text is "The Vaccine Safety Handbook," *Parents Educating and Advocating for our Children's Health*, https://s3.amazonaws.com/assets.forward.com/downloads/measles-vaccine-peach-magazine-pdf-brooklyn-1554905824.pdf. For information on measles vaccinations in Indonesia, see Dyna Rochmyaningsih, "Indonesian Fatwa Causes Immunization Rates to Drop," *Science* 362, no. 6415 (2018): 628–629.

6 For a systematic analysis of moral intuitions and antivax attitudes, see Avnika B. Amin, Robert A. Bednarczyk, Cara E. Ray, Kala J. Melchiori, Jesse Graham, Jeffrey R. Huntsinger, and Saad B. Omer, "Association of Moral Values with Vaccine Hesitancy," *Nature Human Behaviour* 1 (2017): 873–880.

7 Malcolm Gladwell, *Blink: The Power of Thinking without Thinking* (New York: Little, Brown, 2005); Richard A. Posner, "Blinkered," *The New Republic*, January 23, 2005, https://newrepublic.com/article/68000/blinkered.

8 *The Thinker* photograph is public domain, from www.metmuseum.org/art/ collection/search/191811.

9 Daniel Kahneman, *Thinking, Fast and Slow* (New York: Farrar, Straus, and Giroux, 2011).

10 Amos Tversky and Daniel Kahneman, "Judgment under Uncertainty: Heuristics and Biases," *Science* 185, no. 4157 (1974): 1124–1131.

11 Amos Tversky and Daniel Kahneman, "Availability: A Heuristic for Judging Frequency and Probability," *Cognitive Psychology* 5, no. 2 (1973): 207–232.

12 Amos Tversky and Daniel Kahneman, "Extensional versus Intuitive Reasoning: The Conjunction Fallacy in Probability Judgment," *Psychological Review* 90, no. 4 (1983): 293–315.

13 Adam Carlson, "Trump Celebrates Autism Awareness Day … After Years of Falsely Claiming Vaccines Cause Autism," *People*, April 2, 2019, https://people.com/politics/donald-trump-autism-awareness-day-vaccines-tweet/.

14 Kurt Gray and Daniel M. Wegner, "Moral Typecasting: Divergent Perceptions of Moral Agents and Moral Patients," *Journal of Personality and Social Psychology* 96, no. 3 (2009): 505–520.

15 Tage S. Rai and Daniel Diermeier, "Corporations Are Cyborgs: Organizations Elicit Anger but not Sympathy When They Can Think but Cannot Feel," *Organizational Behavior and Human Decision Processes* 126 (2015): 18–26.

16 Jonathan L. Fischer and Aaron Mak, "The Evil List," *Slate.com*, January 15, 2020, https://slate.com/technology/2020/01/evil-list-tech-companies-dangerous-amazon-facebook-google-palantir.html.

17 Michael Barbaro and Justin Gillis, "Wal-Mart at Forefront of Hurricane Relief," *The Washington Post*, September 6, 2005, www.washingtonpost.com/archive/business/2005/09/06/wal-mart-at-forefront-of-hurricane-relief/6cc3a4d2-d4f7-4da4-861f-933eee4d288a/.

18 Arthur S. Jago and Jeffrey Pfeffer, "Organizations Appear More Unethical than Individuals," *Journal of Business Ethics* 160, no. 1 (2019): 71–87.

19 Jonathan Haidt, *The Righteous Mind: Why Good People Are Divided by Politics and Religion* (New York: Pantheon Books, 2012). As with many theories in the behavioral sciences, there is debate over this theory. See, for example, Christopher L. Suhler and Patricia Churchland, "Can Innate, Modular 'Foundations' Explain Morality? Challenges for Haidt's Moral Foundations Theory," *Journal of Cognitive Neuroscience* 23, no. 9 (2011): 2103–2116.

20 Jesse Graham, Jonathan Haidt, and Brian A. Nosek, "Liberals and Conservatives Rely on Different Sets of Moral Foundations," *Journal of Personality and Social Psychology* 96, no. 5 (2009): 1029–1046.

21 Jonathan Haidt, *The Righteous Mind: Why Good People Are Divided by Politics and Religion* (New York: Pantheon Books, 2012).

22 Stephanie Innes, "State Rep. Kelly Townsend Says Mandatory Vaccinations are 'Communist,'" *AZCentral.com*, February 28, 2019, www.azcentral.com/story/news/local/arizona-health/2019/02/28/state-rep-kelly-townsend-says-mandatory-vaccinations-communist/3018342002/.

23 David G. Rand and Ziv G. Epstein, "Risking Your Life without a Second Thought: Intuitive Decision-Making and Extreme Altruism," *PLoS One* 9, no. 10 (2014); Mordecai Paldiel, "The Face of the Other: Reflections on the Motivations of Gentile Rescuers of Jews," www.yadvashem.org/righteous/

resources/the-face-of-the-other-reflections-on-the-motivations-of-rescuers .html.

24 For a thorough analysis of Intel's conflict minerals policy, see Sheila Melvin and Ken Shotts, "Looking Inside: Intel and Conflict Minerals," *Stanford Graduate School of Business Case ETH-5*, 2015. The Krzanich quotation is from "The Road to Conflict-Free," *Mashable.com*, October 29, 2014, https:// mashable.com/2014/10/29/conflict-free-minerals/.

25 Gina Bellafante, "'We Didn't Sign Up for This': Amazon Workers on the Front Lines," *The New York Times*, April 3, 2020; Paul Blest, "Leaked Amazon Memo Details Plan to Smear Fired Warehouse Organizer: 'He's not Smart or Articulate,'" *Vice News*, April 2, 2020, www.vice.com/en/article/5dm8bx/ leaked-amazon-memo-details-plan-to-smear-fired-warehouse-organizer-hes-not-smart-or-articulate; Bernie Sanders, Twitter post, April 1, 2020, https:// twitter.com/SenSanders/status/1245466894540382208.

26 Julia Angwin, Surya Mattu, and Jeff Larson, "The Tiger Mom Tax: Asians Are Nearly Twice as Likely to Get a Higher Price from Princeton Review," *Pro Publica*, September 1, 2015, www.propublica.org/article/asians-nearly-twice-as-likely-to-get-higher-price-from-princeton-review.

27 David E. Broockman, Gregory Ferenstein, and Neil Malhotra, "Predispositions and the Political Behavior of American Economic Elites: Evidence from Technology Entrepreneurs," *American Journal of Political Science* 63, no. 1 (2019): 212–233.

28 David Broockman and Joshua Kalla, "Durably Reducing Transphobia: A Field Experiment on Door-to-Door Canvassing," *Science* 352, no. 6282 (2016): 220–224.

29 Matthew Feinberg and Robb Willer, "The Moral Roots of Environmental Attitudes," *Psychological Science* 24, no. 1 (2013): 56–62.

Chapter 3

1 Jessica Livingston, 2007, *Founders at Work: Stories of Startups' Early Days* (New York: Apress, 2007); James Gleick, "How Google Dominates Us," *The New York Review of Books*, August 18, 2011; Josh McHugh, "Google vs. Evil," *Wired*, January 1, 2003.

2 Richard Lawler, "Alphabet Replaces Google's 'Don't Be Evil' with 'Do the Right Thing,'" *Engadget*, October 2, 2015, www.engadget.com/2015-10-02-alphabet-do-the-right-thing.html.

3 "2019 College Admissions Bribery Scandal," *Wikipedia, the free encyclopedia*, last updated January 5, 2021, https://en.wikipedia.org/wiki/2019_college_admissions_bribery_scandal.

4 Leon Festinger, *A Theory of Cognitive Dissonance* (Stanford, CA: Stanford University Press, 1957).

5 See also: Mark D. Alicke and Olesya Govorun, "The Better-Than-Average Effect," in Mark D. Alicke, David Dunning, & Joachim Krueger (eds.), *The Self in Social Judgment* (New York: Psychology Press, 2005).

6 Constantine Sedikides, Rosie Meek, Mark D. Alicke, and Sarah Taylor, "Behind Bars but above the Bar: Prisoners Consider Themselves More Prosocial Than Non-Prisoners," *British Journal of Social Psychology* 53, no. 2 (2014): 396–403.

7 Benoît Monin and Dale T. Miller, "Moral Credentials and the Expression of Prejudice," *Journal of Personality and Social Psychology* 81, no. 1 (2001): 33–43.

8 Daniel A. Effron, Jessica S. Cameron, and Benoît Monin, "Endorsing Obama Licenses Favoring Whites," *Journal of Experimental Social Psychology* 45, no. 3 (2009): 590–593.

9 John A. List and Fatemeh Momeni, "When Corporate Social Responsibility Backfires: Theory and Evidence from a Natural Field Experiment," *Management Science* 67, no. 1 (2021): 8–21.

10 "Ex-CEO Scrushy Ordered to Pay HealthSouth Shareholders $3B," *USA Today*, June 19, 2009.

11 Jerry Parkinson, *Infractions: Rule Violations, Unethical Conduct, and Enforcement in the NCAA* (Lincoln, NE: University of Nebraska Press, 2019); Jake New, "Two Decades of 'Paper Classes,'" *Inside Higher Ed*, October 23, 2014.

12 Dan Kane, "Deborah Crowder's Story Could Bring NCAA Investigators to UNC," *Charlotte News Observer*, April 15, 2014, www.charlotteobserver .com/news/local/education/article9113093.html.

13 John Carreyrou, *Bad Blood: Secrets and Lies in a Silicon Valley Startup* (New York: Alfred A. Knopf, 2018).

14 Clayton M. Christensen, "How Will You Measure Your Life?" *Harvard Business Review* 88, nos. 7–8 (2010): 46–51.

Chapter 4

1 Frank Langfitt, "NUMMI," *This American Life*, July 17, 2015; John Shook, "How to Change a Culture: Lessons from NUMMI," *MIT Sloan Management Review*, January 1, 2010; Benjamin Gomes-Casseres, "NUMMI: What Toyota Learned and GM Didn't," *Harvard Business Review*, September 1, 2009.

2 Lee Ross, "The Intuitive Psychologist and His Shortcomings: Distortions in the Attribution Process," in Leonard Berkowitz (ed.) *Advances in Experimental Social Psychology*, vol. 10 (New York: Academic Press, 1977).

3 John M. Darley and C. Daniel Batson, "'From Jerusalem to Jericho': A Study of Situational and Dispositional Variables in Helping Behavior," *Journal of Personality and Social Psychology* 27, no. 1 (1973): 100–108.

4 Stanley Milgram, *Obedience to Authority: An Experimental View* (New York: Harper & Row, 1974).

5 Robert B. Cialdini, Linda J. Demaine, Brad J. Sagarin, Daniel W. Barrett, Kelton Rhoads, and Patricia L. Winter, "Managing Social Norms for Persuasive Impact," *Social influence* 1, no. 1 (2006): 3–15.

6 Alan S. Gerber and Todd Rogers, "Descriptive Social Norms and Motivation to Vote: Everybody's Voting and so Should You," *The Journal of Politics* 71, no. 1 (2009): 178–191.

7 Lee Ross, David Greene, and Pamela House, "The 'False Consensus Effect': An Egocentric Bias in Social Perception and Attribution Processes," *Journal of Experimental Social Psychology* 13, no. 3 (1977): 279–301.
8 Francis J. Flynn and Scott S. Wiltermuth, "Who's with Me? False Consensus, Brokerage, and Ethical Decision Making in Organizations," *Academy of Management Journal* 53, no. 5 (2010): 1074–1089.
9 Aaron Beam, interview with Mike Hochleutner (Stanford), November 2010.
10 Dale T. Miller and Cathy McFarland, "When Social Comparison Goes Awry: The Case of Pluralistic Ignorance" in Jerry M. Suls & Thomas Ashby Wills (eds.), *Social Comparison: Contemporary Theory and Research* (Hillsdale, NJ: Lawrence Erlbaum Associates, Inc., 1991).
11 For a more detailed discussion of the LIBOR scandal, see Sheila Melvin and Ken Shotts, "Barclays and the LIBOR: Anatomy of a Scandal," Stanford Graduate School of Business Case ETH-03, 2013.
12 "Parks, Rosa," The Martin Luther King, Jr. Research and Education Institute at Stanford University, https://kinginstitute.stanford.edu/encyclopedia/parks-rosa.
13 Interview with Jo Ann Robinson for *Eyes on the Prize: America's Civil Rights Years (1954–1965)*, August 27, 1979, Washington University Libraries, Film and Media Archive, http://digital.wustl.edu/e/eop/eopweb/rob0015.0530 .090judyrichardson.html.
14 Ian Ayres and Cait Unkovic, "Information Escrows," *Michigan Law Review* 111 (2012): 145–196.

Chapter 5

1 Specialization and the organization of production is a classic topic of interest to economists. Our example of production of a book is inspired by Leonard E. Read, "I Pencil: My Family Tree As Told to Leonard E. Read," *The Freeman* 8, no. 12 (1958): 32–37. Read's example of a pencil was popularized in Milton Friedman and Rose D. Friedman, *Free to Choose: A Personal Statement* (New York: Harcourt Brace Jovanovich, 1980).
2 Gallup survey responses to the question "Next, we'd like to know how you feel about the state of the nation in each of the following areas. For each one, please say whether you are – very satisfied, somewhat satisfied, somewhat dissatisfied or very dissatisfied. If you don't have enough information about a particular subject to rate it, just say so. How about – the size and influence of major corporations?", accessed January 2021, https://news.gallup.com/poll/5248/big-business.aspx.
3 All quotations from Smith in this chapter are from Adam Smith, *An Inquiry into the Nature and Causes of the Wealth of Nations*, 1776.
4 Milton Friedman, "A Friedman Doctrine: The Social Responsibility of Business is to Increase Its Profits," *New York Times Magazine*, September 13, 1970.
5 From Schulz's comments in a fifty-year retrospective on Friedman, "Greed Is Good. Except When It's Bad," *Dealbook/The New York Times Magazine*, September 13, 2020.

6 Oliver Hart and Luigi Zingales, "Companies Should Maximize Shareholder Welfare Not Market Value," *Journal of Law, Finance, and Accounting* 2, no. 2 (2017): 247–274.
7 David P. Baron, "Corporate Social Responsibility and Social Entrepreneurship," *Journal of Economics, Management, and Strategy* 16, no. 3 (2007): 683–717.
8 Board of Governors of the Federal Reserve System, "DFA: Distributional Financial Accounts, assets by wealth percentile group in 2020: Q1," accessed January 2021, www.federalreserve.gov/releases/z1/dataviz/dfa/compare/chart/#quarter:122;series:Assets;demographic:networth;population:all;units:levels.
9 For an extensive discussion of the political economy of financial regulation, see Anat R. Admati, "It Takes a Village to Maintain a Dangerous Financial System," in Lisa Herzog (ed.), *Just Financial Markets? Finance in a Just Society* (Oxford: Oxford University Press, 2017).
10 The companies spent at least $57 million (Uber), $52 million (Doordash), $49 million (Lyft), $32 million (InstaCart), and $13 million (Postmates). Jeong Park, "Uber, Lyft and Allies Break Spending Records on Gig Worker Initiative. Here's How Much." *The Sacramento Bee*, October 24, 2020.
11 Data from OpenSecrets.org, accessed January 2021, www.opensecrets.org/federal-lobbying/summary and www.opensecrets.org/federal-lobbying/top-spenders.
12 LobbyFacts.eu, "Crowding the Corridors of Power: Corporate Lobbyists Outnumber NGOs and Unions in the European Parliament by 60%," accessed January 2021, https://lobbyfacts.eu/articles/30-01-2017/crowding-corridors-power-corporate-lobbyists-outnumber-ngos-and-unions-european.
13 Alexander V. Hirsch and Kenneth W. Shotts, "Competitive Policy Development," *American Economic Review* 105, no. 4 (2015): 1646–1664; Alexander V. Hirsch and Kenneth W. Shotts, "Policy-Development Monopolies: Adverse Consequences and Institutional Responses," *The Journal of Politics* 80, no. 4 (2018): 1339–1354.
14 Rebecca Henderson, *Reimagining Capitalism in a World on Fire* (New York: Hachette, 2020); Lynn A. Stout, *The Shareholder Value Myth: How Putting Shareholders First Harms Investors, Corporations, and the Public* (San Francisco: Berrett Keohler Publications, 2012); Ian I. Mitroff, *Stakeholders of the Organizational Mind* (San Francisco: Jossey-Bass, 1983); R. Edward Freeman, *Strategic Management: A Stakeholder Approach* (Englewood Cliffs, NJ: Prentice-Hall, 1984).
15 Laurence D. Fink, Memorandum to CEO's, January 2018, www.nytimes.com/interactive/2018/01/16/business/dealbook/document-BlackRock-s-Laurence-Fink-Urges-C-E-O-s-to-Focus.html?dlbk.
16 Business Roundtable, *Statement on the Purpose of a Corporation*, 2019, https://s3.amazonaws.com/brt.org/BRT-StatementonthePurposeofaCorporationOctober2020.pdf.
17 Benioff quotations are from his comments in a fifty-year retrospective on Friedman, "Greed Is Good. Except When It's Bad," *Dealbook/The New York Times Magazine*, September 13, 2020.

18 Lynn Stout, "Corporations Don't Have to Maximize Profits," *NYTimes.com*, April 16, 2015, www.nytimes.com/roomfordebate/2015/04/16/what-are-corpor ations-obligations-to-shareholders/corporations-dont-have-to-maximize-profits.

19 Leo E. Strine, Jr., "The Dangers of Denial: The Need for a Clear-Eyed Understanding of the Power and Accountability Structure Established by the Delaware General Corporation Law," *Wake Forest Law Review* 50, no. 3 (2015): 761–793.

20 Michael E. Porter and Mark R. Kramer, "Creating Shared Value. How to Reinvent Capitalism – and Unleash a Wave of Innovation and Growth," *Harvard Business Review* (January–February 2011): 62–77.

21 Salesforce Press Release, "Salesforce Announces Strong Second Quarter Fiscal 2021 Results," August 25, 2020, www.salesforce.com/news/press-releases/ 2020/08/25/salesforce-announces-strong-second-quarter-fiscal-2021-results/.

22 Josh Rivera, "Salesforce Notifies Employees of Around 1,000 Job Cuts amid Stock Surge," *USA Today*, August 26, 2020.

23 Peter S. Goodman, "Big Business Pledged Gentler Capitalism. It's Not Happening in a Pandemic," *The New York Times*, April 13, 2020.

24 Lawrence H. Summers, "If Business Roundtable CEOs are Serious about Reform, Here's What They Should Do," *The Washington Post*, September 2, 2019.

25 Andrew Ross Sorkin, "A Company Backs a Cause. It Funds a Politician Who Doesn't. What Gives?," *The New York Times*, September 22, 2020, www .nytimes.com/2020/07/21/business/dealbook/corporate-political-donations .html.

26 Niraj Chokshi and Michael S. Schmidt, "Boeing Reaches $2.5 Billion Settlement with U.S. Over 737 Max," *The New York Times*, January 7, 2021.

27 Anat R. Admati, "It Takes a Village to Maintain a Dangerous Financial System," in Lisa Herzog (ed.), *Just Financial Markets? Finance in a Just Society* (Oxford: Oxford University Press, 2017).

28 Cary Funk and Meg Hefferon, "U.S. Public Views on Climate and Energy," *Pew Research Center*, November 25, 2019, www.pewresearch.org/science/ 2019/11/25/u-s-public-views-on-climate-and-energy/.

Chapter 6

1 Joshua Greene, *Moral Tribes: Emotion, Reason, and the Gap between Us and Them* (New York: Penguin Press, 2013).

2 Angela Chang (DoorDash Head of Brand), "Celebrate Earth Day with DoorDash and Plant a Tree," April 22, 2016, https://medium.com/ @DoorDash/celebrate-earth-day-with-doordash-and-plant-a-tree- d3cf4e45f595.

3 Jennifer Maloney, "Juul Raises $650 Million in Funding That Values E-Cig Startup at $15 Billion," *The Wall Street Journal*, July 10, 2018.

4 Betsy McKay, Jennifer Maloney, and Anne Marie Chaker, "Juul to Stop Sales of Most Flavored E-Cigarettes in Retail Stores," *The Wall Street Journal*, November 9, 2018.

5 The question of measurement was a key point of disagreement between Bentham and Mill. Bentham did not distinguish between different forms of happiness or pleasure, whereas Mill argued that certain pleasures were more valuable than others. See "The History of Utilitarianism," *The Stanford Encyclopedia of Philosophy*, https://plato.stanford.edu/entries/utilitarianism-history/#JerBen.

6 John Stuart Mill, *On Liberty* (Boston: Fields, Osgood & Company, 1859).

7 Philippa Foot, "The Problem of Abortion and the Doctrine of the Double Effect," *Oxford Review* 5 (1967): 5–15; Judith Jarvis Thomson, "The Trolley Problem," *Yale Law Journal* 94, no. 6 (1985): 1395–1415.

Chapter 7

1 Our description of the opioid epidemic in this chapter draws on Sheila Melvin and Ken Shotts, "The Opioid Epidemic," Stanford GSB Case ETH-18 (A), 2019.

2 Travis Reider interview by Terry Gross, "Motorcycle Crash Shows Bioethicist the Dark Side of Quitting Opioids Alone," *Fresh Air*, July 8, 2019, www.npr.org/transcripts/738952129.

3 Agreed Statement of Facts, *United States of America v. The Purdue Frederick Company Inc.*, US District Court of the Western District of Virginia Abingdon Division, 2007, www.documentcloud.org/documents/5744917-Purdue-2007-Agreed-Statement-of-Facts.html.

4 Office of Xavier Becerra Press Release, "Attorney General Becerra Sues Opioid Manufacturer Purdue Pharma for Its Illegal Practices and Role in the Opioid Crisis," June 3, 2019.

5 In Deep with Angie Coiro (April 18, 2020). Susan Fowler–Whistleblower: My Journey to Silicon Valley and Fight for Justice at Uber. Audio Podcast. https://podcasts.apple.com/gb/podcast/in-deep-with-angie-coiro-interviews/id1004182626.

6 Katy Waldman, "The Confidante's Dilemma," *Slate.com*, November 1, 2017.

7 Cork Gaines and Shayanne Gal, "Colleges Spend More Money on Coaches than Scholarships for Student-Athletes," *Business Insider*, March 12, 2019; James Crabtree-Hannigan, "Dabo Swinney, Nick Saban and the 10 Highest-Paid College Football Coaches in 2019," *SportingNews.com*, January 13, 2020.

8 Rohan Nadkarni, "Why a Large Group of Pac-12 Players Are Prepared to Sit Out the Football Season," *SI.com*. August 2, 2020.

9 "College Football is not Essential," *The New York Times*, August 29, 2020.

Chapter 8

1 Jonathan Haidt, "Of Freedom and Fairness," *Democracy: A Journal of Ideas* 28 (2013): 38–50.

2 David Kass, "Warren Buffett's Meeting with University of Maryland MBA Students," December 8, 2013, http://blog.umd.edu/davidkass/2013/12/08/

warren-buffetts-meeting-with-university-of-maryland-mbams-students-novem
ber-15-2013/.

3 World Bank Press Release, "Nearly Half the World Lives on Less Than $5.50 a
Day," October 17, 2018.

4 For a thorough response to this critique see John Rawls, *Political Liberalism*
(New York: Columbia University Press, 1983).

5 Robert D. Putnam, "E Pluribus Unum: Diversity and Community in the
Twenty-First Century," *Scandinavian Political Studies* 30, no. 2 (2007):
137–174.

6 Zaid Jilani, "The 'Diversity' Trap," June 29, 2020, *Tablet*, www.tabletmag
.com/sections/news/articles/the-diversity-trap-jilani.

Index